SEXUAL SLAVERY IN AMERICA

SEXUAL SLAVERY
IN AMERICA

BY ADOLPH F. NIEMOELLER
B.S., A.B., M.A.

Fredonia Books
Amsterdam, The Netherlands

Sexual Slavery in America

by
Adolph F. Niemoeller

ISBN: 1-58963-787-9

Reprinted from the 1935 edition

Fredonia Books
Amsterdam, The Netherlands
http://www.fredoniabooks.com

TABLE OF CONTENTS

vii

VI

APPENDICES

FOREWORD

Erotology and sexology, as recognized, discrete sciences or branches of science, are as yet of no great age: some of the pioneers in the fields are still living and there are none of them dead long enough to have become truly famous. But in this rather short space of time sexology, or more broadly, erotology, has emerged from obscurity, passed through persecution and taboo, and achieved a fair degree of tolerance and general interest.

But in this process the field of the science's subject matter appears to have become pretty well circumscribed and fixed—frozen, one might almost say. Antiquity, and particularly classical antiquity, has received a large share of the erotologist's attention, and the major portion of his residual efforts seem to have been focused on nineteenth century western Europe. And even further, the great bulk of these studies have been only in the sphere of sexual abnormality, of perversion and perversity, in the realms of aberration, anomaly, and curiosity. Strange as it may seem, erotology (I use the broader term) is not solely a matter of sexual psychopathology; the latter is but a phase, a branch of the former. There is as much, if not more, to be learned from and about the normal and near-normal manifestations of the sex instinct and its concomitant activities as there is from its gross, frightful, startling excesses and aberrations. Some small attempt, I confess, has been made to envisage sexual phenomena in their broader, human, sociological, and national aspects—most notably by Iwan Bloch,—but as yet the tendency is very feeble and limping.

The present volume combines attempts at two very faltering steps in the indicated desirable directions. For one thing, for about the first time in the history of erotology we have a study of a sexual question taking its locale in America, a country which for some reason has heretofore been rather slighted by erotologists. And in addition we here have something of a novelty in erotologic literature in the consideration of a single, definite phase of sexuality, namely, sexual slavery. Ordinarily, sexual phenomena have been studied in the large, as cross-sections of a period, country, or people, in which a little of a great variety of things appear. But here it has been essayed to follow one single issue of a country's sex life through the history of that country and to study its genealogy and anatomy as thoroughly as possible. If in future years we shall have a great number of similar studies of other aspects of sexuality, we shall be in a position to begin deducing the fundamental principles and hypotheses of erotology that are always necessary to elevate a line of study to the dignity of a true science.

How well I have succeeded in my double effort remains to be seen; it is not for me to judge of that. But poor as my attempt may be, I plead for at least sufferance in view of my endeavor, weak as it is, to lead erotology into channels of more profitable activity.

However, together with the above, I feel that the book in hand presents an interesting and enlightening examination, and in the main represents work in an original direction. True, white slavery, the burden of one of the sections herein, has been frequently written about and described, but here I hope to have sifted out most of the irrelevant details and to have presented a reasonably, orderly and adequate picture of the situation. The treatment of the other phases of sexual slavery is, so far as I know, entirely original.

In closing, I wish to acknowledge my indebtedness to my friend Esar Levine for his aid in securing many data for my chapter on white slavery and to thank him most sincerely, both for his help and for his friendship.

St. Louis, Mo.   A.F.N.
April, 1935.

SEXUAL SLAVERY
IN AMERICA

I

INTRODUCTION

THOUGH there is no indisputable, or even good, supporting evidence, it is generally conceded that prostitution is the oldest profession; by the same token I presume we may take it that slavery is the oldest institution. And in truth, just as prostitution shows itself as well-established, even venerable, at the earliest origins of recorded history, likewise does slavery. The Old Testament certainly treats it as no novelty and Homer takes it quite as a matter of course.

However, our interest here is not slavery, but sexual slavery and the sexual aspects of slavery, and this again, I daresay, rivals the other two in antiquity. Few persons, I hazard, could long have absolute control of the life and body of another person without the sexual implications of the situation obtruding themselves. Property rights and sexual rights have ever been man's two most immediate and vital concerns, and with the slave's position as property once settled his possibilities as a sexual organism would not likely long remain unscrutinized. But let there be no mistake: undoubtedly the initial purpose behind the taking and holding of slaves was utilitarian or economic, a useful bit of machinery to do necessary work or produce profit for the master, but the sexual phase of slavery, though secondary to the other, has, I feel sure, been concomitant to the other and present in varying degrees from the start, particularly when it concerned female slaves. Though there can be no evidence to support such a view, still it seems to be implicit in the very situation and logically to be inferred from it. Few women can long be even to a small extent subject to a man's will without the question of their sexual complaisance arising. Present-day instances of affairs between kitchen maids and the men of the household are too numerous to require detailing here, but they do bear witness to the immutability of human nature throughout the ages and lend weight to my contentions, while it has become axiomatic that no woman who makes any least pretense of decency and respectability will accept money or any sort of real favor from a male as such obligation is currently accepted as implying but one result.

That the effects of slavery—the effects not only on the slave but also on the master and on the society and manners of the time in general—were on the whole demoralizing, seems little to be disputed by students of the question. In speaking of ancient slavery as an institution, Ingram is quite definite on this point:

"In its action on the slave it marred in a great measure the happy effects of habitual industry by preventing the development of the sense of human dignity which lies at the foundation of morals, whilst the culture of his ideas and sentiments was in most cases entirely neglected, and the spontaneous education arising from the normal family relations was too often altogether denied him. On the morality of the masters—whether personal, domestic, or social—the effects of the institution were disastrous.

"The habit of absolute rule, always dangerous to our nature, was peculiarly corrupting when it penetrated every department of daily life, and when no external influence checked individual caprice in its action on the feelings and fortunes of inferiors. It tended to destroy the power of self-command, which is the first principle of all moral progress; whilst it exposed the master to the baneful influences of flattery. As regards domestic morality, the system offered constant facilities for libertinism; we cannot doubt that the female slave was often sacrificed to the brutality of the master, or radically corrupted when perhaps scarcely more than a child. It tended to subvert domestic peace by compromising the just dignity and ruining the happiness of the wife. The morality of the sons of the family was early undermined, and the general tone of feeling of the younger generation lowered by their intimate association with a despised and degraded class."[1]

But even more than this, the institution of slavery seems to affect and corrupt the very fiber and structure of the society and country in which it exists, fostering and even engendering practises and abuses which paradoxically enough turn back and degrade the institution whence they sprung. As for example, certain forms of prostitution can arise only from a condition of slavery,

[1] John Kells Ingram, *A History of Slavery and Serfdom*, London, 1895, pp. 9-11.

and this prostitution will unavoidably misuse the slaves under it and darken the name of slavery. Lecky, the great historian, attributes the utter and thoroughgoing depravity of ancient Roman life and society in large part to the prevalence of slavery. "In addition to its manifest effect in encouraging a tyrannical and ferocious spirit in the masters," he says, "it cast a stigma upon all labor, and at once degraded and impoverished the free poor. In modern societies the formation of an influential and numerous middle class, trained in the sober and regular habits of industrial life, is the chief guarantee of national morality, and where such a class exists, the disorders of the upper ranks, though undoubtedly injurious, are never fatal to society... The aristocracy may revel in every excess of ostentatious vice, but the great mass of the people, at the loom, the counter, or the plow, continue unaffected by their example, and the habits of life into which they are forced by the condition of their trades preserve them from gross depravity. It was the most frightful feature of the corruption of ancient Rome that it extended through every class of the community. In the absence of all but the simplest machinery, manufactures, with the vast industrial life they beget, were unknown. The poor citizen found almost all the spheres in which an honorable livelihood might be obtained wholly or at least in a very large degree preoccupied by slaves, while he had learned to regard trade with an invincible repugnance. Hence followed the immense increase of corrupt and corrupting professions, as actors, pantomimes, hired gladiators, political spies, ministers to passion, astrologers, religious charlatans, pseudo-philosophers, which gave the free classes a precarious and occasional subsistence, and hence, too, the gigantic dimensions of the system of clientage. Every rich man was surrounded by a train of dependants, who lived in a great measure at his expense, and spent their lives in ministering to his passions and flattering his vanity... Ionian slaves of a surpassing beauty, Alexandrian slaves, famous for their subtle skill in stimulating the jaded senses of the confirmed and sated libertine, became the ornaments of every patrician house, the companions and instructors of the young... The slave population was itself a hotbed of vice, and it contaminated all with which it came in contact." [2]

But we have ample evidence to attest to the sexual abuses of slavery, and it shall be the purpose of the following pages to consider these abuses in a general, representative manner, particularly as affecting America, as well as to survey what was the sexual life, both in its coercive and restrictive aspects, of the slaves in bondage, and finally to study sexual slavery in the various forms in which we find it present in our country. Thus, to sum it up tersely, our theme is sexual slavery and the sexual life of slaves.

The structure of sexual slavery as a whole is obviously very complex and inter-related, with its issues constantly crossing, paralleling, and merging. But for the sake of more expeditiously envisaging the matter it is advisable

[2] Wm. E. H. Lecky, *History of European Morals,* 3rd ed., rev., N. Y., 1918, vol. I, pp. 262-263.

to divide the subject into logical categories, however arbitrary such an arrangement must of necessity be. Therefore, I suggest the following scheme:

I. CHATTEL SLAVERY.

In this the slave *belongs* to the master, is his property, and his body, will, movements, and the expression of his appetites and impulses are entirely and absolutely subject to the will and whim of the master. Sexual slavery under this condition may be of two sorts:

(a) *Immediate.* Sexual license of the master toward the slaves, forced concubinage, promiscuous and unbridled relations with them, perverted or sadistic practises toward them, etc.

(b) *Indirect.* Control by the master or master class of the sexual affairs of the slaves, prohibitions against or coercion toward their matings and marriages, forced breeding of slaves for profit, and in general legislating and regulating their sex life, even to the point of considering sex crimes committed by them or on them totally differently in law courts from similar crimes committed by free persons.

II. DOCTRINAL SLAVERY.

By this is intended those cults, sects, organizations, or schemes of a religious, political, economic, or merely fanatic nature, in which one of the sexes (almost always the female) is to a greater or lesser degree subjugated to the will of the other in sexual matters, that is, subjugated to a greater extent than is the case under the law and custom of the people round about, as with the Mormons, the Oneida Community, etc. Naturally, the whole institution of religious or sacred prostitution comes in this division. As this branch of the subject, though extremely interesting, has never at any period affected any noteworthy percentage of the American population, as have the other forms of bondage subsequently treated, it shall be omitted from this volume.

III. COERCIVE SLAVERY.

Here it is a question of the holding of women—by physical force, fraud, trickery, or in any illegal fashion—to a mode of sexual life against their inclination and will. In America the category becomes practically identical with white slavery and shall so be treated in this study.

IV. ECONOMIC SLAVERY.

Under this heading is grouped those practises or modes of behavior in which or through which a person (usually a woman) lives a sexual life with a person of opposite sex only by reason of certain financial considerations or obligations. This again falls into two classes:

(a) *Conventional.* In this class we find all those marriages which are legal enough as marriages go, but in which one mate has married the other and endures him and his advances only because of the pecuniary aspects of the situation. This also includes the whole system of marriage brokerage. Here there is no physical coercion, but there has been a most patent bartering in bodies, which constitutes an essential feature of slavery. There must be no confusion between this and free prostitution in which there is a general sale to all comers of a woman's body for that woman's living, for in the former case the sale is to one man, or master, and a mere living is rarely a pressing consideration in the matter, though frequently a *better* living is.

(b) *Unconventional.* Here we have the whole matter of mistresses, kept women, and the like, where women are living with men and granting them their sexual favors out of wedlock by reason of such money or support as they derive from the union. There is nothing indigenous, or even peculiar, to the American soil in this practise, and consequently it will not be treated in this volume.

V. TRADITIONAL SLAVERY.

This is meant to describe a variety of bondage which, though in some cases made legal by law, gets its chief force and sanction through the customs and traditions of the people and country. It takes on a double aspect:

(a) *Marital Slavery.* Though not readily apparent to the casual observer, a wife, and also a husband to a great extent, is by our marriage laws, customs, and usages so constrained and restricted in her sexual conduct, various powers being given her mate over her, and such penalties are imposed for any derelictions or failings, that her condition, and in particular her sexual condition, is decidedly reminiscent of that of a chattel slave.

(b) *Promiscuous Slavery*. This condition is present primarily among primitive peoples (as, for example, some American Indian tribes) and makes any woman fair prey to any man who can catch her away from protection—the protection of her home, a male relative, or the like—and overcome her. This is not to be confused with mere rape, for where such usage prevails the man is entirely within his rights in his actions and is liable to no one. Not very many centuries ago in the large European cities decent women would not venture on the streets after dark as roving bands of young blades would be out seeking just such opportunities.

VI. PSYCHIC SLAVERY.

This last category brings us to a totally different situation. In all the above divisions of sexual slavery, the slave was subject to another because of external circumstances, that is, external to himself, objective. But here we have the opposite case in which the "slave" is so for subjective reasons, because of a warping, maladjustment, or perversion of the instincts, and particularly of the sexual instincts. In this condition the person's libido has become so malassociated that it cannot be aroused or gratified unless he is meanly, basely, or cruelly treated, as one would a slave, by a beloved person, or sometimes by any person. The will of such an unfortunate is entirely subservient to that of the dominating person. Such an affliction may be evidenced as masochism, pageism, flagellomania, etc. As this is an universal phenomenon and not one peculiar to America, it will receive no further treatment in the present work.[8]

Be it understood that the above classification is only my own tentative attempt logically to arrange the subject matter in hand, and that it is entirely possible that other, and better, cataloguings could readily be devised. However, in the absence of a better this may be taken as a fair scheme of the anatomy of our subject and will serve to supply the reader with some conception of the ramifications of a question whose implications and manifestations have heretofore been given scarcely any notice. Naturally, it will not be advisable to study sexual slavery in America according to the above outline, as each phase of its occurrence here involves a blending of several of the basic aspects listed. Instead we shall study our problem historically, taking it up in the various forms under which it became prominent at different periods, and to this we shall now pass, after first pausing for a brief glance at the historical background of sexual slavery.

[8] For data on masochism and allied phenomena, see Krafft-Ebing, *Psychopathia Sexualis;* Iwan Bloch, *The Sexual Life of Our Time;* Dr. Jacobus X——, *The Abuses, Aberrations and Crimes of the Genital Sense;* Albert Moll, *Perversions of the Sex Instinct;* etc. See also the novel *Venus in Furs* by Leopold von Sacher-Masoch, whence this aberration gets its name.

II

SEXUAL SLAVERY IN ANTIQUITY

VOLTAIRE, who said a great many things, has among them proclaimed: "Slavery is also as ancient as war, and war as human nature." If we match this with rather an obvious parallel statement: Sexual license and abuse is as old as the power of one person over another, and knead the two together, we with little difficulty discover that: Sexual slavery is as old as human nature, which makes it very old indeed. And, in truth, what is probably the oldest grudge we have a record of, that of Achilles against Agamemnon as related in the first book of the *Iliad,* bears out both of the above contentions, for Achilles becomes angry and pouts through a great part of the Trojan War because Agamemnon, his king, takes from him the fair maid Briseis, the plaything of his lighter moments, who was his portion of the spoils of an earlier battle. And it has been going on ever since that time.

The fighting man would quite expectedly take as slaves only desirable females for three chief reasons: to minister to his lusts; to attend his daily, personal needs and tasks; and because they would not be nearly so dangerous as male, enemy slaves. "In the hunter period the savage warrior does not enslave his vanquished enemy, but slays him; the women of a conquered tribe he may, however, carry off and appropriate as wives or servants, for in this period domestic labor falls almost altogether on the female sex."[4] So it would seem that the course of the matter has run thusly: that at first women were enslaved primarily because of their being women and that the labor angle of the situation, while present, was secondary; whereas when labor grew increasingly important, slavery extended to men, or included men and women indiscriminately, and the sexual angle, though present, became secondary.

Slaves and slavery were common enough among the ancient Hebrews to warrant there being not a few dicta concerning their treatment laid down in the Old Testament,[5] not neglecting points of a sexual nature. "The Hebrew slave was to be set free after a servitude of six full years, leaving behind him, however, the wife whom his master might have given him during that period, and any children she had borne him. If he was married when he was enslaved (as a debtor), then they both went free."[6] It seems that in general the position of the maid-servant was much the same as that of the man-servant. Though frequently the concubine of the master, she was often the particular property of the mistress, perhaps

[4] J. K. Ingram, *op. cit.*, pp. 1-2.

[5] The chief declarations concerning slaves can be found at *Exodus*, 20:17; 21:2-11; and 21:20 ff.

[6] J. K. Ingram, *op. cit.*, p. 266.

having been given to her at marriage.[7] "A female slave, whom her father had sold in consequence of poverty, was similarly to be set free in the seventh year. If the master had made her his concubine and publicly recognized her as such, he could not, if he afterwards repudiated her, sell her; if he had made her his son's concubine, he was obliged to treat her as a daughter. If he kept her to himself, but took another with her, he must give her all the prerogatives of a half-wife—'food, raiment, and duty of marriage'; otherwise, he must set her free."[8] But, on the whole, the lot of the Hebrew slave appears not to have been excessively severe; in fact, wives, too, were originally purchased from the parents, and wives and concubines are frequently difficultly distinguishable,[9] so it is likely that the slave lived under no more severe conditions than the average wife.

In ancient Greece, in the early days before her subjection and degradation when honor was yet more than a name, the ministering to the mass lust of the people at large, while held to be an inescapable necessity, was considered as rather mean and certainly not the worthy occupation of a free Greek woman. Hence, the common whores of that time were almost without exception foreign slave women, and even the higher-class free courtesans, while including many Greek women, were largely of foreign birth and freed slaves. LaCroix (Pierre

[7] *Dictionary of the Bible,* James Hastings, ed., N. Y., 1918, art. "Slave, slavery."

[8] J. K. Ingram, *op. cit.,* p. 266.

[9] *Dictionary of the Bible,* James Hastings, ed., *loc. cit.*

Dufour) sums up the situation regarding ancient Greek prostitution: "There were three principal classes...: the *Dicteriades,* the *Auletrides,* and the *Hetairai.* The first were, in a manner, the slaves of Prostitution; the second were its auxiliaries; the third were its queens." [10] Solon, the great Athenian law-giver of the late seventh and early sixth centuries B.C., wishing to provide for the protection of Greek womanhood by supplying ready outlets for man's natural lusts, as well as to divert into the State's coffers some of the revenues being heaped up by the temples through their religious prostitution, founded public houses of prostitution (*dicteria*) in which he placed large numbers of slave women (*dicteriades*), purchased with State funds, to act as prostitutes and to serve, without power of refusal, the needs and desires of any one paying the nominal fee fixed by the State, namely, one obole (about three cents). [11] In speaking of these *dicteriades,* Sanger declares that: "This class approaches more nearly than any other to the prostitutes of our day, the main difference being that the former were bound by law to prostitute themselves when required to do so, on the payment of the fixed sum, and that they were not allowed to leave the state." [12] These *dicteriades* were in the main poor captives who were bought up outside of Greece and gathered together from

[10] Paul LaCroix (Pierre Dufour), *History of Prostitution,* trans. by Samuel Putnam, Chicago, 1926, vol. I, p. 97.

[11] *Ibid.,* p. 85.

[12] Wm. W. Sanger, *The History of Prostitution,* N. Y., 1913, p. 47.

all countries by agents for that business.[13] This applies, of course, only to the true slave prostitutes; there were also not a few low Greek women who would voluntarily assume the position of a *dicterias* for various reasons. Says LaCroix: "The dicteriades who were shut up were almost always foreign women, slaves who had been purchased here, there and everywhere by a speculator; the free dicteriades, on the contrary, were Greeks whom vice, idleness, or misery had caused to fall into this degree of abasement and who endeavored, with a remnant of modesty, to conceal the degrading trade by which they lived."[14] These latter women, while strictly not slaves, nevertheless had the status of slaves and lost their rights of citizenship. Then, too, there were speculators who owned numbers of slaves and would hire them out for various uses as occasion demanded, for labor, entertainment, prostitution, etc.[15] "There were also public slaves; of these some belonged to temples, to which they were presented as offerings, amongst them being the courtesans who acted as *hierodules* at Corinth and at Eryx in Sicily."[16]

The whole pattern of sacred prostitution is but a specialized form of sexual slavery: the bodies of women are dedicated to the meretricious service of a god or goddess, with no power of refusal, and the revenues from their devotional commerce goes—usually *in toto*—not to them-

[13] LaCroix, *op. cit.*, vol. I, p. 123.

[14] *Ibid.*, p. 111.

[15] J. K. Ingram, *op. cit.*, p. 21.

[16] *Ibid.*, p. 21.

selves but to the temple. This institution dates back to remote antiquity; Herodotus, writing in the fifth century B.C., reports that: "The Babylonians have one most shameful custom. Every woman born in the country must once in her life go and sit down in the precinct of Venus, and there consort with a stranger...lines of cord mark out paths in all directions among the women, and the strangers pass among them to make their choice. A woman who has once taken her seat is not allowed to return home until one of the strangers throws a silver coin in her lap, and takes her with him beyond the holy ground. When he throws the coin he says these words— 'The goddess Mylitta prosper thee.' (Venus is called Mylitta by the Assyrians.) The silver coin may be of any size; it cannot be refused, for that is forbidden by the law, since once thrown it is sacred. The woman goes with the first man who throws her money, and rejects no one. When she has gone with him, and so satisfied the goddess, she returns home, and from that time forth no gift however great will prevail with her...A custom very much like this is found also in certain parts of the Island of Cyprus." [17]

But the Babylonians were by no means alone in the practise of such curious rites. "The Mylitta of Chaldea became Astarte in Phœnicia, at Carthage, and in Syria. Nothing was changed but the name; the voluptuous rites were identical. In addition to the forced prostitution of the temples, however, the Phœnicians and most of

[17] Herodotus, *Clio*, 199, trans. by George Rawlinson. This same custom is also mentioned by Baruch, vi, 43.

their colonies maintained for many years the practise of requiring their maidens to bestow their favors on any strangers who visited the country. Commercial interest, no doubt, had some share in promoting so scandalous a custom. On the high shores of Phœnicia, as at Carthage and in the island of Cyprus, the traveler sailing past in his boat could see beautiful girls, arrayed in light garments, stretching inviting arms to him."[18] One might travel where he would in those times, Armenia or Egypt, Media, Persia, or Parthia, and whether they were the *hierodules* of Corinth or the *pellices* of Thebes, at almost every place would he find numerous slave-prostitutes, either religious or civic, ready to do his bidding on payment of the standard fee.[19] Strabo (xii, 532) declares that: "What the Medes and Persians regard as sacred, is also honored among the Armenians; but amongst them the cult of Anaïtis flourishes most. For her young male and female slaves prostitute themselves. That is not astonishing, but even the most distinguished persons in the land sell their maiden daughters, and the law orders that they must not wed until they have served the goddess a long time, without anyone disdaining them as wives."[20]

[18] Wm. W. Sanger, *op. cit.,* p. 42.
[19] G. S. Wake, in his essay *Sacred Prostitution* treats further of all this. This essay may be found in his *Serpent Worship,* or in L. A. Stone's *The Story of Phallicism,* as well as elsewhere. See also, J.-A. Dulaure, *The Gods of Generation,* chap. X.
[20] Cited in Hans Licht, *Sexual Life in Ancient Greece,* trans. by J. H. Freese, N. Y., 1932, p. 392.

In Greece, naturally, sacred prostitution was no less prevalent than in the countries round about. Strabo (viii, 6) informs us that in the city of Corinth alone there were a thousand female slaves attached as public courtesans to the temple of Aphrodite.[21] Pindar has left us an eulogy to Xenophon of Corinth, a contender in the Olympian Games of 464 B.C., on the occasion of the fulfilling of this man's vow that in the event of his success he would dedicate a hundred courtesans to the services of the temple of Aphrodite in that city. At the ceremony of their dedication, the hundred women danced in the temple while the words of the eulogy were sung:

"Guest-loving girls! servants of Suasion in wealthy Corinth! ye that burn the golden tears of fresh frankincense, full often soaring upward in your souls unto Aphrodite, the heavenly mother of Loves. She hath granted you, ye girls, blamelessly to cull on lovely couches the blossom of delicate bloom; for, under force, all things are fair...

"O Queen of Cyprus! a herded troop of a hundred girls hath been brought hither to thy sacred grove by Xenophon in his gladness for the fulfillment of his vows..."[22]

Among the later Romans, of course, most institutions and principles broke up pretty thoroughly on the rocks of egotism and wanton lust, but even so, sacred prosti-

---

[21] Cited in W. G. Holmes, *The Age of Justinian and Theodora*, London, 1905, p. 330; also in Wake, *Sacred Prostitution*.

[22] *The Odes of Pindar*, trans. by Sir John Sandys, The Loeb Classical Library, N. Y., 1927, pp. 581-583.

tution was still carried on among them to an extent. "We also shall find that sacred prostitution existed in Sicily in the temple of Venus Ericyna. Slave women were attached to this temple, and these prostituted themselves, as at Corinth and in Asia, half for the profit of the altar, half for themselves, until such time as they had acquired enough money to obtain their ransom and liberty. The worship of Venus Ericyna was a celebrated one, but under Tiberius her temple was deserted and fell into ruin. This Emperor finally restored it and peopled it with female slaves, charged with the functions of the priestesses of Venus." [28]

This practise is found further exemplified in India, not only in antiquity but even in quite recent times. The Abbé Dubois, writing at about the start of the eighteenth century, informs us that: "The courtesans or dancing girls attached to each temple take their place in the second rank; they are called *devadasis* (servants or slaves of the gods), but the public call them by the more vulgar name of prostitutes. And in fact they are bound by their profession to grant their favors, if such they be, to anybody demanding them in return for ready money. It appears that at first they were reserved exclusively for the enjoyment of the Brahmins. And these lewd women, who make a public traffic of their charms, are consecrated in a special manner to the worship of the divinities of India. Every temple of any importance

[28] Edmund Dupouy, *Prostitution in Antiquity*, in *The Story of Phallicism*, L. A. Stone, Chicago, 1927, vol. II, p. 501.

includes in its service a band of eight, twelve, or more."[24]

But except for sacred prostitution, the organized, large-scale, State-controlled prostitution of slave women seems to have fallen off as Greece gradually disintegrated, and at Rome it appears never to have been an important, clearly discernible single issue. Prostitution there was in Rome aplenty, particularly in somewhat later times, but it was isolated to no especial class or caste, extending from the Empresses down to the meanest slaves. Naturally, there were speculators, male and female, who exploited the bodies of a group of slaves they owned, but this has been true of all times and countries—even including in a revised form present-day America—and is not closely comparable to the conditions of ancient Greece. True, the average Roman would not have dreamt of disdaining an attractive slave girl, but then he would not have disdained any attractive girl regardless of her estate: he saw the female and not her condition. The individual purchase of female slaves to pamper lust went on, of course, in Rome just as it did much later in our own South, but again, I repeat, sexual slavery in our particular sense could hardly be considered to have been a national institution in old Rome. Cato the Censor, stern Cato himself, it is asserted by Livy (xxxiv), cohabited with a female slave for some time after the death of his first wife; in fact, it is said that he married a second wife only to avoid a scandal as a result of this commerce. However, there was no

[24] Abbé J. A. Dubois, *Hindu Manners, Customs and Ceremonies*, trans. by H. K. Beauchamp, 3rd ed., Oxford, 1928, pp. 584-585.

absence in Rome of secondary sexual slavery, of legislation and control of the sex life of slaves. "Law still refused in general to recognize the marriage of slaves; but Justinian gave them a legal value after emancipation in establishing rights of succession. Unions between slaves and free women, or between a freeman and the female slave of another, long continued to be forbidden, and were even punished in certain circumstances with atrocious severity. But it was provided that the marriage of a master with his freed-woman enfranchised and legitimized their children born in slavery, and, even without marriage, if a female slave had lived with her master as wife till her death, her children were free." [25] Even the actual sexual acts of slaves were rarely considered in the same light as those of free persons: "A female slave was still held incapable of the offense of adultery; but Justinian visited with death alike the rape of a slave or freed-woman and that of a free maiden." [26] We had this same sharp distinction in the legal sexual status in the courts and law in our own South in the days of Negro slavery.

In Europe during the Middle Ages, and even later, the feudal lords had powers which included certain features of sexual slavery, as their ability to bring about, prohibit, or regulate the marriage and mating of their serfs, and more especially as regards their rights with the brides under their domain. This privilege is known by various names, but most commonly by those of *jus*

[25] J. K. Ingram, *op. cit.*, pp. 68-69.
[26] *Ibid.*, p. 69.

cunni or *jus primæ noctis*. Under these privileges it was required, on pain of rather severe penalties and fines, that all newly married brides under a lord's suzerainty had to be brought on their wedding night to the lord's bedchamber and he be the one to deflower them, their husbands having no opportunity with them until the second night. Though the lord would often take merely a fee from the husband as a substitute, he nevertheless had full power to claim the bride's virginity.[27]

Among the Mohammedans slavery has long been an accepted institution, and it is Koranic law that they be treated fairly and humanely. Nevertheless, the master has unquestioned, and even legal, sexual rights over his slaves. I shall allow a Mussulman scholar and student of Koranic law to speak:

"The power of the master over his slaves is absolute. He can employ them in such service or such work as seems good to him. He can dispose of them at his will...

"The master likewise has the right of giving his slaves in marriage to whom it seems good to him; but he cannot order them to separate when they are married. No more has he the right of authorizing two of his slaves, male and female, to live together in concubinage.

"The children of slaves belong to the master of the mother.

"A patron may cohabit with his female slaves; but it

[27] See J.-A. Dulaure, *The Gods of Generation*, chap. XV, for further details of this practise. See also E. Westermarck, *The History of Human Marriage*, chap. V, for quite a full discussion and criticism of the matter.

is not permitted him to have coition with mother and daughter, with two sisters, with aunt and niece, or with the near relatives of his slaves. If, living with the one, he permits himself the least liberty with the other, he violates the law of Islam and his double commerce is a double crime. I add that it is not permitted a Mussulman to cohabit with a pagan slave." [28] The condition of Mohammedan concubine-slaves among modern (19th century) Egyptians is detailed at some length by Lane. [29]

And with this we shall conclude our very meager and somewhat sketchy survey of the history of sexual slavery and pass on to our study of such conditions in America, leaving it for those who are especially interested in the points touched upon above to prosecute their further researches in the directions suggested by the references.

[28] Omer Haleby, *El Ktab, or the Book of the Secret Laws of Love,* bk. II, chap. I.
[29] E. W. Lane, *The Manners and Customs of the Modern Egyptians.* See, for example, Everyman's Library ed., pp. 100, 103, 136, 190, etc.

III

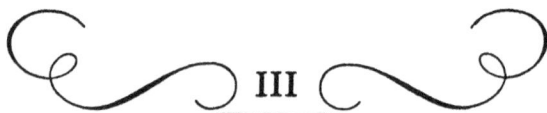

SEXUAL SLAVERY AMONG THE AMERICAN INDIANS

THE popular conception of the "noble redskin" as a walking embodiment of natural nobility, inherent chivalry, and relative sexual dispassionateness, has become a legend of proportions fit almost to rank with that of the colossal absence of mendacity on the part of the Father of Our Country. But despite the frequent reiteration of this estimate by many popular writers on Indian customs and character, such a judgment finds little support among men who have any great knowledge of the Indian at first hand, or for that matter of primitive peoples in general. A writer who has spent a small lifetime among the American Indians declares: "I have been at pains to show that the Indian has not only no moral code, but that he has not the faintest conception of an idea of moral obligation. This is exemplified not only in their general customs, but in their individual everyday life.

"For the man there is no such word, no such idea, as continence. He has as little control over his passions as any wild beast, and is held to as little accountability for their indiscriminate gratification. Of all the tribes that I know of, Indian men are the same."[30]

Though the degree of disparity is not quite as great, we find the same difference of opinion regarding the condition of the Indian woman. The average person has long taken it for granted that the squaw is entirely subject to the male, having no will of her own and little choice in her movements or actions. However, we find it stated that: "The condition of women among the Indians of America has long been misunderstood and, when considered at all, frequently placed in an erroneous light, the female usually being regarded as a slave and drudge ᴸᴏth before and after her marriage. This misconceived view, due largely to inaccurate observation, may possibly have been correct in some isolated cases and particularly among certain tribes possessing but few of the elements of social organization, especially those which were non-agricultural...As a rule the woman was looked upon by the men of the tribe as their equal...In nearly all tribes possessing rudiments of social organization, woman was sole master of her own body. Violation of their own 'r alien women was rare and regarded with horror and aversion."[31]

But this is the typical viewpoint of the scholar, the writer who forms his opinions by the more or less un-

[30] Col. R. I. Dodge, *Our Wild Indians: Thirty-three Years Personal Experience Among the Red Men of the Great West,* Hartford, Conn., 1882, p. 210.
[31] W. H. Miner, *The American Indians North of Mexico,* Cambridge, 1917, pp. 35-38.

balanced selection from the reports of others, many of whom themselves are in turn not first-hand investigators. It is usually quite another matter with the writer who has himself been the observer of the subject of his report, and it is this latter category, I feel, that should receive the greater amount of credence. Such an one is Col. Dodge, whose estimate of the squaw's position follows:

"The life of an Indian woman is a round of wearisome labor. Her marriage is only an exchange of masters, and an exchange for the worse, for the duties devolved upon a girl in the parental lodge are generally of the lightest kind...All her labors...are in or near the family lodge, and where she is immediately under the eyes of her parents. For an unmarried girl to be found away from her lodge alone, is to invite outrage, consequently she is never sent out to cut and bring wood, nor to take care of the stock...As a rule all the hard outdoor work devolves upon the married women.

"The pride of the good wife is in permitting her husband to do nothing for himself. She cooks his food, makes and mends his lodge and his clothing, dresses skins, butchers the game, dries the meat, goes after and saddles his horse...

"The husband owns his wife entirely. He may abuse her, beat her, even kill her without question. She is more absolutely a slave than any Negro before the war of the rebellion, for not only may herself, but her person be sold or given away by her husband at his pleasure and without her consent." [82] The inferences anent her sexual

[82] R. I. Dodge, *op. cit.*, pp. 204-205.

status are not difficult to be drawn from such complete subjugation. Nor is the above merely an isolated opinion on the inferiority of Indian women. No less an authority than Catlin affirms: "So far as I have yet traveled in the Indian country, I have never yet seen an Indian woman eating with her husband. Men form the first group at the banquet, and women and children and dogs all come together at the next."[33] This inferior, really servile, condition of woman seems to have been pretty generally the rule throughout the North American Indians. "Amongst the Iroquois tribes the men ate first and by themselves, then the women and children took their meals alone. Of these people it has been said that the women 'must approach their lords with reverence; they must regard them as exalted beings, and are not permitted to eat in their presence.' So amongst many other tribes of North American Indians."[34]

The Indian wife was in the majority of cases a mere chattel of the husband; she had to be bought from her father and could be sold, exchanged, or bartered at the will of her husband. The sale of a wife by the husband was not at all unusual, especially if she proved infertile and bore no offspring within a reasonable length of time.[35] One of the prime reasons for early marriage

[33] G. Catlin, *Illustrations of the Manners, Customs, and Conditions of the North American Indians,* London, 1876, vol. I, p. 202.
[34] Ernest Crawley, *The Mystic Rose,* rev. by Theo. Besterman, N. Y., 1927, vol. I, pp. 205-206.
[35] R. I. Dodge, *op. cit.,* p. 213. The custom of wife selling has had some currency in most parts of the world at various times. The

among Indian girls is the fact that the father was as a rule eager to realize as soon as possible on her value by receiving the "bride price" her prospective husband had to pay to purchase her for himself. "Sometimes a father gets 'hard up' and has to sell his girls while they are yet mere children. These are bought up cheap by well-to-do bucks, who give them, even while mere children, all the rights and privileges as wives.

"San-a-co, a Comanche chief, and the best Indian from our standpoint that I have ever known, had as wife a pretty little maid of ten years, of whom he was very fond.

"In March, 1880, 'Red Pipe,' a Cheyenne, sold his little unformed daughter of eleven years, to be the wife of a man old enough to be her grandfather; and I have known several other warriors who have mere children as their third or fourth wives."[36] So profitable can this bride selling be that old and ugly widows can often get another husband merely by giving him proprietorship of their daughters, not as wives, but as so much negotiable property.[37] The fact of a father's often being able to get perhaps twice as much for his daughter from a white man as from an Indian, has led to many cases of selling to the highest bidder, and the Indians have been dismayed and have complained bitterly over the number

novelist Thomas Hardy recounts such a transaction in England in his *Mayor of Casterbridge*.

[36] *Ibid.*, pp. 216-217. For rather a full treatment of the subject of bride price, purchase, exchange, etc., see E. Westermarck, *The History of Human Marriage*, chap. XXIII.

[37] *Ibid.*, p. 217.

of abandoned wives, widows, and orphans left on their
hands as a result of such bartering, but the father always
insisted on his right to dispose of his daughters as he
saw fit.[38]

The squaw was ever disposed of in the most brusque
of manners; she had, in the parlance of today, to "take
it and like it." Her conduct, her movements, her person,
or her will were not her own. "The Northern Indians
sometimes exchanged wives for a night. It was esteemed
as one of the strongest ties of friendship."[39] Thus the
wives would be passed about by the men willy-nilly
merely as a token of their mutual friendliness, with scant
regard for the feelings or sentiments of the women. But
then, in many tribes any woman was considered the fair
prey of any man; all that was necessary was that he manage in some way to obtain possession of her. "A Cheyenne
woman, either married or single, is never seen alone.
Though any man has the right to assault her, she is
required to protect herself, and this can only be done by
always having some one with her."[40] So widespread was
the accepted license and right of assault of the men over
the women that among the Plain tribes in general, and
among the Cheyennes and Arapahoes in particular, the
women had a most curious custom devised to protect
themselves. "No unmarried woman considers herself
dressed to meet her beau at night, to go to a dance, or

[38] *Ibid.,* p. 218.
[39] E. Crawley, *op. cit.,* vol. I, p. 297.
[40] R. I. Dodge, *op. cit.,* p. 213.

other gathering, unless she has tied her lower limbs with a rope, in such a way, however, as not to interfere with her powers of locomotion; and every married woman does the same before going to bed when her husband is absent. Custom has made this an almost perfect protection against the brutality of the men. Without it, she would not be safe for an instant, and even with it, an unmarried girl is not safe if found alone, away from the immediate protection of her lodge." [41] This is a curious and interesting variation of the medieval chastity belt.

So much for the customary servile and subject estate of the Indian woman, a condition of which sexual slavery was a logical and very real component; let us now turn to slavery proper among the Indians. Slavery in America is commonly construed as being a matter solely of the Negro in the old South; it is but rarely realized that there was considerable Indian slavery in early Colonial times before it was replaced by the more suitable Negro slavery. Moreover, there was slavery among the Indians themselves before the arrival of the white man. "Le Jeune found the Huron and Ottawa Indian slaves engaged in minor household duties. In the northwest, enslaved women and children performed the same labor. One other use to which the young women and girls were put, if they did not marry into the tribe, was to serve as the mistresses of their owners." [42] The institution of

[41] *Ibid.,* pp. 212-213.
[42] Almon Wheeler Lauber, *Indian Slavery in Colonial Times Within the Present Limits of the United States* (vol. 54 of

slavery by the Indians appears to have had some existence throughout America, but in particular on the
Northwest Coast. "Perhaps all the tribes of North
America were accustomed to take captives in war. Among
the people of the Plains the lot of these captives was
generally an easy one. The women and girls were married into the tribe of their captors and their children
took their places as equals in the community... In contrast, the tribes on the Pacific Coast kept such captives
in slavery, allowing them to mate only with each
other, and continuing their descendants in slavery per-
petually... Socially and politically, they had no standing,
and were classed as chattels."[48]

A peculiar variation of Indian-imposed Indian slavery,
occurring sporadically throughout America, was what
might be termed *homosexual slavery*. Perhaps this phenomenon is best known in that class of persons among the
Mexicans, and also the Pueblos of New Mexico, that went
under the name of *mujerados*. These were men who
were especially selected to be dedicated to the practise
of passive sodomy and to that end were deliberately made
effeminate by excessive horseback riding and masturba-
tion repeated several times daily, which eventually resulted in the atrophy of their genitals, and their
consequent impotence, and often even more or less complete loss of the male secondary sexual characteristics.

Columbia University's "Studies in History, Economics and Public Law"), N. Y., 1913, p. 36.
[48] P. E. Goddard, *Indians of the Northwest Coast*, N. Y., 1924,
p. 85.

Passive sodomy was the profession of these persons; they had no choice.[44]

But the Mexicans were not at all alone in the effeminating of certain males especially dedicated to this purpose. Frazer speaks of a "custom widely spread among savages, in accordance with which some men dress as women and act as women throughout life...Often they are dedicated and trained to their vocation from childhood. Effeminate sorcerers and priests of this sort are found among the Sea Dyaks of Borneo, the Bugis of South Celebes, the Patagonians of South America, and the Aleutians and many Indian tribes of North America."[45] Among the Sioux there was a particular man, the *berdashe* or *i-coo-coo-a,* who dressed and lived as a woman and who was the recipient of a yearly festival. "For extraordinary privileges which he is known to possess, he is driven to the most servile and degrading duties, which he is not allowed to escape; and he, being the only one of the tribe submitting to this disgraceful degradation, is looked upon as 'medicine' and sacred and a feast is given to him annually."[46] Primitive peoples throughout the world have had similar practises.[47]

[44] Iwan Bloch, *The Sexual Life of Our Time,* trans. by M. E. Paul, N. Y., 1928, pp. 426, 544-545; Dr. Jacobus X——, *Crossways of Sex,* chap. II.

[45] Sir. J. G. Frazer, *The Golden Bough,* London, 1911-1915, 3rd ed., vol. VI, p. 253.

[46] G. Catlin, *op. cit.,* vol. II, pp. 214-215.

[47] See Crawley, *The Mystic Rose,* vol. II, pp. 101ff., for a lengthy discussion of this forced inversion of boys and men among many tribes and peoples.

But Indian slavery was by no means restricted to that imposed by the Indians themselves; the white man, on his arrival, was not slow to follow their example, as witness the action of the Spaniards. "Soto had the foresight, before setting out on his journey of exploration, to provide guides, consisting of Indian slaves seized in the territory which he expected to traverse, and seized others to act in this capacity as occasion required. Slaves were used for the same purpose by Coronado. The women slaves were used largely as cooks and as mistresses. Soto apportioned women slaves among his men. The narrators relate the capture and distribution of such women in groups of one hundred to three hundred. Women were sometimes given by the chiefs to the white men for this purpose, as in the case of Coronado's expedition." [48] Nor were the Spaniards the sole offenders in this matter; the French, naturally, soon followed in their footsteps. "Early in the eighteenth century, life among the French of Louisiana, both rich and poor, was quite licentious, and one of the means of fostering this life was the use of Indian women, slave and free. The demoralization resulting from such a condition attracted attention, and in 1709 it was urged that girls suitable for wives be sent over in order 'to prevent these disorders and debaucheries.' " [49] This advice was followed, with certain logical abuses, as we shall see.

Indian slavery continued well on into Colonial times, paralleling the later institution of white servitude, until

[48] A. W. Lauber, *op. cit.,* p. 55.
[49] *Ibid.,* p. 83.

eventually it, as I have already mentioned, along with the other, was replaced by Negro slavery as being infinitely better adapted to meet the labor requirements of the New World. Of course, the sexual phase of slavery underwent a corresponding alteration.

IV

SEXUAL SLAVERY IN COLONIAL TIMES AND AMONG INDENTURED SERVANTS

COLONIAL America was on all counts a crude, coarse, unfeeling place to live; it lent itself but poorly to the flowering forth of sentiments and emotions, either those of love and affection or of an economic or business nature. Self betterment and promotion was the keynote of life in those times, as perhaps it still largely is, but then it was so virtually to the complete exclusion of all other, gentler aspects of life and human intercourse. This was true not only among the Colonists, but perhaps was even more viciously fostered by schemers and promoters back in the mother countries, particularly in England. Human life, bodies, emotions, sensibilities, and the like, were as nothing in their eyes beside the cold reality of hard cash; these human features and traits of the poor unfortunates in their power were constantly exploited but never considered. Families were separated, girls violated, children starved, mistreated, beaten, all in the interest of return on the investment. Naturally, the American Colonists of any affluence or position were not slow themselves to regard their less fortunate brothers in a similar light.

In the early days, the colony of Virginia was practically all one large plantation owned by the London Company. This organization had promised its settlers and stock-holders great things, but had defaulted miserably; consequently, in 1619 a new, representative management was formed which tried various measures for getting the company on a sound basis and putting the Colonists on a firmer, more contented footing. "While granting lands liberally, the company continued to send servants to cultivate reserved lands on public account; it procured shiploads of young women to marry the bachelors and stop their longing for England as home... The maidens found eager embrace by the bachelors and widowers alike who had wearied of womanless life."[50] These girls came on the whole of impoverished families, or were orphan and destitute and embarked with the captains of these ships as a last resort. Ordinarily the captains, or the companies they represented, would sell these women to prospective husbands to reimburse themselves for the passage over, to say nothing of netting a nice profit on the transaction in the bargain. Female bodies were bought and sold to steady the foundations of young America!

Often, the more wealthy of the Colonial planters when desiring a wife were not content to take their chances with these job lots that were sent over; commonly, they had quite definite ideas of what they wanted in a woman.

[50] Ulrich B. Phillips, *Life and Labor in the Old South,* Boston, 1929, p. 19.

Planters, being far from centers of supply, ordinarily would commission London merchants to fill their various needs at 2½% on the transaction, so if the need happened to be a wife, what could have been more logical than to turn to the same source to satisfy it? I wish to offer the following negotiation of a West Indian planter as an interesting example of such a piece of business:

"A prospering settler in the West Indies, feeling the need for a wife, ordered from London along with his annual supplies by next ship 'a young woman of the qualifications and form following: As for portion I demand none, let her be of an honest family; between twenty and twenty-five years of age; of a middle stature and well proportioned; her face agreeable, her temper mild, her character blameless, her health good, and her constitution strong enough to bear the change of climate... If she arrives and conditioned as above said, with the present letter endorsed by you,... that there may be no imposition, I hereby oblige and engage myself to satisfy the said letter by marrying the bearer at fifteen days sight.'

"The agent promptly sent a maiden who carried the document endorsed, along with certificates of temper, character and health from neighbors, her curate and four physicians; and in due time the twain were made one."[51] This whole deal is decidedly reminiscent of horse-trading.

But Colonial America knew a yet more real form of slavery before the institution of Negro slavery, a form

[51] *Ibid.*, p. 141.

which naturally carried its sexual restriction and regulation of the bondmen; it is most commonly known as *indentured servitude.* "Negro slavery was not the only sort of bondage known in America in the seventeenth and eighteenth centuries. It was in fact because of a system already in existence that it became permanently fixed in the colonies. This system was known as *servitude* or *indenture*,[52] and it explains many of the early acts with reference to the Negroes, especially those about intermarriage with white people. Servitude was 'a legalized status of Indian, white, and negro servants preceding slavery in most, if not all, of the English mainland colonies.' " [53] The details of the mechanism and magnitude of the trade in indentured servants, as well as of their general status and condition, are a bit beside the point in our discussion here; [54] suffice it to say in definition merely that they were men and women, of all ages, who had wished to come to America from the mother countries and lacking funds had signed up with a ship's captain or a company to labor in the Colonies without wage

[52] This designation derived from the custom of the servant and master both signing the agreement or "indenture" of servitude and then tearing it into two jagged-edged parts (hence the name), one part of which was kept by each party. The validity of each part could be tested by matching its jagged edge with that of the other.

[53] Benj. G. Brawley, *A Short History of the American Negro,* N. Y., 1913, p. 14.

[54] For further, more general, information on indentured servants, see Bruce, *Institutional History of Virginia;* also, James Oneal, *The Workers in American History.*

for a definite number of years in return for their passage over. On reaching the shores of the New World they would then be sold, bartered, or auctioned by the captains or agents of the company without power of choice or refusal on their part, just as actual slaves would have been treated, saving only that their bondage had a time limit. "Unmarried people of both sexes find ready buyers. Old married people, widows and the feeble, are a drug on the market." [55] The best people of the time found nothing shameful in this revolting practise, and even utilized it to their best advantage. That pillar of American liberty, Benjamin Franklin, did not hesitate to turn an honest penny by making capital of the persons of his fellow Americans. "Franklin, when proprietor of the 'Pennsylvania Gazette,' occasionally purchased slaves or the time of redemptioners and advertised them for sale in his paper. 'Likely Negro wenches' were advertised for sale in the same columns with white boys and girls and sometimes, when the trade was not brisk, they were sold at public auction." [56]

These indentured servants were as completely subject to the will and dictates of the master in all things as any slave. "The contract signed, the newcomer *became in the eyes of the law a slave,* and in both the civil and criminal code was classed with Negro slaves and Indians. None could marry without consent of the master or mistress

[55] James Oneal, *The Workers in American History*, 3rd ed., St. Louis, Mo., 1912, p. 84.
[56] *Ibid.*, p. 65. For a list of such advertisements from Franklin's paper, see Heston, *Slavery and Servitude in New Jersey*, pp. 24-25.

under penalty of an addition of one year's service to the time set forth in the indenture." [57] This rigid control of such very personal matters as the matings and marriages of the bondmen was quite general throughout the Colonies, as for example:

"In 1691, Virginia passed an act forbidding the union of free whites with Indians, whether slave or free; but there seems to have been no provision against marriage of Negroes or Indians with white indentured servants. The provision, perhaps, was unnecessary, for the consent of the white indentured servant's master was necessary for the validity of such a union, and such consent was usually refused because of the strong prejudice against race mixture.

"North Carolina, also, in 1715, passed an act forbidding the marriage of whites with Negroes, mulattoes or Indians, under penalty of £50, and making clergymen celebrating such a marriage liable to a fine of £50. A later act of 1741 provided a fine of £50 for the marriage of any white man or woman with an Indian, Negro, mustee, mulatto, or any person of mixed blood to the third generation, bond or free. Any minister or justice of the peace performing such a service was punishable by a fine of £50. Maryland, on its own part, in 1692, passed an act against the marriage or promiscuous sexual relations of whites and Negroes or other slaves. Any white person so offending was to become a servant for seven years, if free at the time of the marriage. If already a servant, he or

[57] McMaster, *The Acquisition of the Political, Social and Industrial Rights of Man in America*, p. 35.

she must serve seven years after the end of the present term of service.

"The same feeling existed in New England. A Massachusetts act of 1692 forbade the marriage, under severe penalty, of any white person with a Negro, Indian or mulatto." [58]

In Maryland, the anti-miscegenation laws seem to have been somewhat abused and perverted to ends other than had been originally intended. "Some of the more degraded type of women servants in Maryland contracted marriages with slaves and a law of 1664 required that such women should serve their masters during the life of their husbands, while the children of such marriages became slaves for life. 'Instead of preventing such marriages, the law enabled avaricious and unprincipled masters to convert many of their servants into slaves.'" [59]

On the other hand, if the servant was a bit clever about it and watched his opportunities, marriage could be made to furnish a most convenient escape from bondage. "Not a few [indentured servants],...shortened service by marrying a master or mistress or some neighbor who would buy and cancel the indenture. For example, William Bullock wrote as to maid-servants:

"'If they come of an honest stock and have a good repute they may pick and chuse their Husbands out of the better sort of people. I have sent over many, but never could keepe one at my Plantation three moneths, except a poore silly Wench, made for a Foile to set off

[58] A. W. Lauber, *op. cit.*, pp. 252-253.
[59] James Oneal, *op. cit.*, p. 60.

beautie, and yet a proper young Fellow must needs have her, and being but new come out of his time and not strong enough to pay the charges I was at in cloathing and transporting her, was content to serve me a twelve Moneth for a Wife.' " [60]

But perhaps the most relevant manner of getting some sort of clear image of sexual license in Colonial times and the sexual condition of the indentured servants (for exact data of this nature is extremely difficult, even impossible, to find, its being a matter of a sort to be hushed up and avoided in any letters, diaries, or writings of the period) is by considering the extent of bastardy, the attitude toward it, and the provisions made for coping with it. It may safely be assumed, I take it, that in an age less fortunate than ours in not being blessed with any degree of perfection in contraceptives, illegitimacy may be taken as a fair index of sexual license.

"One of the commonest offenses in the 17th century was bastardy, due in part to the degraded character of many servants, men and women, who came or were shipped to the colony, and the fact that many of the women were at the mercy of their masters and forced to enter into illicit relations with them. Masters also opposed marriage among the women servants as this often meant an interruption of their work through confinement and the birth and care of children, while the death of the mother meant the loss of the sum invested in her. Their indentures often rendered it difficult to marry. 'Many of this class of women were exposed to improper

[60] Ulrich B. Phillips, *op. cit.*, p. 24.

advances on their masters' part, as they were, by their situation, very much in the power of these masters, who, if inclined to licentiousness, would not be slow to use it.' The work in the fields and barns and associations after their hours of labor also rendered them easy victims of the lowest class of brutalized laborers and masters.'' [61]

There were many acts and laws enacted in an attempt to suppress, or at least keep down, bastardy, but apparently with little success. In Pennsylvania, women who had illegitimate children were punished by extending the time of their servitude.[62] "Numerous laws were passed to punish the crime of bastardy. Anthony Delmasse and Jane Butterfield were each given thirty lashes in 1642 for this crime and separated until legally united. The punishment of women offenders was generally more severe than for men, the latter generally escaping by paying a fine or some other form of punishment. Sometimes the man was only required to appear before the parish church and confess his sin, while the woman was given a brutal whipping. In 1649 a woman was given fourteen lashes, while the father of her child was sentenced to build a bridge across a creek.'' [63] But legislation and penalties seemed of scant avail. " 'After the middle of the [17th] century, the offense of bastardy became more frequent than ever, owing to the rapid increase in the number of female domestic and agricultural servants, who were imported into the colony.' In 1663 fourteen cases

[61] James Oneal, *op. cit.*, p. 56.
[62] Lodge, *History of the English Colonies*, p. 245.
[63] James Oneal, *op. cit.*, pp. 56-57.

were tried in one county at one session of court, and in 1688 at least three servant women of one master gave birth to illegitimate children." [64]

Matters became so bad that finally even the church had to do more than merely to voice doctrinal disapproval. Toward the end of the 17th century church wardens were empowered to bind out illegitimate boys until they were thirty years of age in order to make some proper disposition of them.[65] Nor did their power stop there; in North Carolina it held that: "If a woman servant gave birth to an illegitimate child she was to serve an additional term, and if the master was the father, *then she was sold by the church wardens for the public benefit.*"[66] The vital thing in all this, of course, was to protect the community from the burden of caring for a large number of bastards; the moral issues involved were decidedly secondary. "One important duty of the church wardens was to see that the parish was saved from expense in cases of bastardy. When a female servant gave birth to a child, the father of which was her master, they were authorized to sell her for a period of two years, the sum being paid in tobacco to the parish. Sometimes they compelled the father to give bond that the child would not become a charge of the parish during the servitude of the mother. Sometimes when masters were fined for this offense the violated mothers were required to repay their

[64] *Ibid.,* p. 57.
[65] *Ibid.,* p. 57.
[66] Lodge, *op. cit.,* p. 155.

masters by an extension of their terms of servitude." [67] Of course, just how the supposedly desired moral impetus was to be derived from legislation that permitted a master to obtain such obvious advantages by the seduction of his female servants, is difficultly ascertainable by an impartial eye. "By the acts giving the master additions of time for the birth of a bastard child to his servant, a premium was actually put upon immorality, and there appears to have been masters base enough to take advantage of it." [68]

White servitude continued on well into the 19th century, or, in more ringing terms, "a half century had passed into history since the adoption of the Declaration of Independence, which declared 'all men are free and equal,' and yet the purchase of white flesh had not become extinct." [69] It had no decisive, clear-cut termination, but, like Indian slavery, died out bit by bit as it was gradually replaced, and far surpassed, by the greatly more practicable Negro slavery.

[67] James Oneal, *op. cit.*, p. 57.
[68] Ballagh, *White Servitude in the Colony of Virginia*, p. 79.
[69] James Oneal, *op. cit.*, p. 70.

V

SEXUAL SLAVERY AMONG THE NEGROES OF THE OLD SOUTH

1. *General Features of Negro Slavery*

WHEN we arrive at the matter of Negro Slavery in America we reach a situation which seems to be of a totally different nature, both of kind and degree. Naturally, Negro slavery attained far greater proportions than did any of the preceding, and partially concomitant, varieties of servitude; but more than this, its issues and fundamental features were quite different, that is, different in the eyes of the people, of the master class. The Negro was not merely a captive people enslaved by its conquerors, but he was held by many—and to a large extent still is—to be an inferior race and more or less close to the animals; [70] therefore, it seemed logically no

[70] The Darwinian theory of evolution fortuitously came along quite conveniently to lend support to this contention in the minds of many who did not hesitate to pervert its doctrines to lend weight to their views in this connection: since the darky did not entirely look an animal, but yet obviously was not a human being, he naturally was a transition product of the evolutionary

more than just and proper that the divine white man should subjugate and control him, domesticate him as he had done many species of animals. Again, though the Indian had been of different race and color from those of the white man, these differences had for some reason never been so keenly felt as in the case of the black man; but with the Negro the sense of this difference was extremely active and colored the whole of the white man's attitude and action toward him, particularly in the sexual sphere. It inhibited the free consideration of normal affection, love, and marriage and brought in the whole problem of miscegenation. In truth, whites could and did love and marry Negroes on occasion, but it was always without legal sanction and in the face of public opinion. Consequently, the sexual relations between whites and Negroes were almost entirely irregular, and also in view of the complete power of the former over the latter these relations were quite extensive and frequent. For the rest, where the master's sexual contact with the Negro was not personal, the darky's sexual acts, habits, and behavior, even of a secondary nature—as his marriage and begetting of offspring—were so controlled, restricted, or compelled in a variety of fashions as to make of him a virtual sexual automaton, or (to justify our title) a sexual slave. These statements apply strictly

chain from the ape to man, though naturally he was much closer to the ape end of the chain than to the man end and consequently might just as well be considered an animal. Remnants of this belief reside in a popular slang term for a Negro still current: *monkey*.

in theory only, of course; no rule or regulation can be so stringent as never to be violated, and where they apply to sexual matters these violations become increasingly frequent with the stringency.

The importation of Negro slaves began in a modest way, but soon grew to great proportions. The first shipload of them came to the colony of Virginia in 1619; by 1725 there were 75,000 Negro slaves in all the Colonies, and in 1776 they numbered half a million.[71] Considering the size of the Colonies in those days, these are rather surprising figures.

With such constantly increasing numbers of Negroes present in the Colonies, their position and condition had to be determined upon, and they were not rated very highly or humanely. Though individual masters frequently accorded their slaves kind and just treatment, they were rarely considered as sentient, volitional human beings; law and custom regarded them as real property, subject to the disposal of the master and incapable of autonomous action. "A slave could own no property unless by sanction of his master, nor make a contract without his master's approval. His mating was mere concubinage in law, though in case of subsequent emancipation it would become a binding marriage. The rape of a female slave was not a crime, but a mere trespass upon the master's property!"[72] The rights and privileges of the slave were negligible, little more, in fact, than

[71] Frederic Bancroft, *Slave-Trading in the Old South,* Baltimore, 1931, p. 2.
[72] Ulrich B. Phillips, *op. cit.,* p. 162.

it was to the master's advantage to grant him for the extraction of the most profitable labor from him. Each colony, and later each state had its own slave code, differing in minor details from each other but all possessing the same general characteristics. "The slave was by law due support in age or sickness, a right to limited religious instruction, and the privileges of marrying, having some free time, and testifying in cases concerning other slaves. If he did not get what was due him he had no redress, for he had no legal voice. His marriage was not considered binding and he was not supposed to have any morals." [73] Truly, the Negro slave was not in any manner pampered or highly rated as an individual.

Now, reaching the more intimate and shameful aspects of our Negro slavery, its sexual features, connections, and abuses, it must be confessed that it is often found necessary to read between the lines in order to get a picture of things. Such matters do not readily find their way into books, diaries, letters, or any records or writings of the period, and indeed but rarely into accounts of the period written at a much later date. The attitude of a German writer as expressed in his prefatory statement to his treatment of the condition of the slave woman in our South, has been all too common in the great generality of literature on American slavery: "The task lying before us has proven to be so devastating and shameful in its manifold aspects that we are compelled henceforward, because of morality and esthetics, to bear the burden of conservatism in the matter of the strange aberrations of

[73] B. G. Brawley, *op. cit.*, p. 55.

the 'Beast Man.'"[74] Consequently, we shall be forced on the whole to piece together rather scattered bits of all too meager data in order to form an opinion on this subject.

We have already noted the fact of the erotic stimulation provoked in the master class by its complete power over the body of the slave; an equally important factor relevant to the subject in hand is the absence in the Negro of morality in our present sense of the word and his possession of a warm, sensual, uninhibited temperament.[75] "It can hardly be denied that Negroes have a comparatively low standard of morals, and any discussion of the violations of the moral code, from the standpoint of the whites, is apt to be colored by the conception of the latter-mentioned race. There can be no question but that miscegenation has declined during the post-bellum period, and emancipation, with the race problem, has been a contributing factor toward preserving the purity of the white race. A traveler wrote in the forties that 'Licentiousness is at its highest tide among the slaves of the South. Amalgamation, adultery, fornication, and incest exist to a deplorable extent. There are no restraints whatever upon these crimes; and I have never heard of their even being reproved for the commission of them. The female slave has no inducement to be chaste—nay, she can have but a very dim and imperfect idea of what

[74] Dr. Joachim Welzl, *Das Weib als Sklavin*, Vienna, 1929, p. 79.
[75] For rather a good account of the moral character and habits of the Negro as a race, as well as of the mulatto, and for a fair amount of data on miscegenation in the South, see A. B. Hart, *The Southern South*, N. Y., 1910.

female purity is; for she has been accustomed to see a promiscuous cohabitation indulged in; and her person is the only means by which she can gain favours, purchase presents, or buy indulgences of any kind...To be the favorite of her master, his son, the overseer, or any white man—or even to be the mistress of the driver,[76] is an honour; and for one so fortunate as she is considered, occupies a post of distinction and preferment.'...The English traveler, Buckingham, states that in no place he had visited in the United States did he find as much immorality and depravity among the slave population as he did in Athens [Georgia]. That masters encouraged their slaves to bear children by bestowing especial favors and gifts needs no substantiation; the records abound with evidence. Data upon concubinage are more difficult to find, but certainly it did exist. Private immorality is not a subject for individuals to note in journals and diaries."[77] The lewdness and open immodesty of the Negroes became so objectionable in Columbus, Georgia, that the following editorial appeared in one of its newspapers: "Our city is too infested with many trifling, idling, vagabond Negro men and women, who will not work for a living, but who resort to gambling, stealing, and prostitution for a living. The worst feature in this is the fact that persons owning houses will rent them to such Negroes, while other white men are found who will

[76] A sort of foreman, himself a Negro and a slave, in charge of a group of slaves.

[77] Ralph B. Flanders, *Plantation Slavery in Georgia*, Chapel Hill, N. C., 1933, p. 270.

cheerfully act as guardians for them...In certain localities of our city, white men and women are forced from necessity to live next door neighbors to prostitute Negro wenches and Negro families who hire their time." [78]

However, let it not for a moment be thought that the Negroes had a monopoly of immorality and absence of shame; Southern planters are notorious for their brutally indecent attitude toward their female slaves and their total lack of respect for any human sensibilities that they might perchance possess. A Tennessee law case bears this out: "Britain v. State, 3 Humphreys 203, July, 1842. 'Indictment charged that...1840..."Britain did...commit...notorious lewdness by...causing and permitting his slaves to go about...so naked and destitute of clothing, that their organs of generation and other parts... which should have been clothed and concealed, were publicly exposed." Proof...that the slave was seen on various occasions...almost entirely destitute of clothing, with some tattered rags hanging upon her, and her body exposed indecently...verdict of guilty...judgment against the defendant, that he pay a fine of $25 and cost,' affirmed." [79]

The white man's brutal, unfeeling attitude toward the slave, and particularly toward the female slave, is further exemplified in his well-known callous thoroughness in the intimate examination of a Negress before pur-

---

[78] *Columbus Weekly Sun*, Aug. 2, 1859, cited by R. B. Flanders, *op. cit.*, p. 271.

[79] Helen T. Catterall, ed., *Judicial Cases Concerning American Slavery and the Negro*, Washington, D. C., 1929, vol. II, p. 515.

chase. "It was both less common and less essential [than in the case of male slaves] thoroughly to inspect the women and the girls, although it was not rare to do so. In any case, it was considered important to know how many children a young woman had borne and what the probabilities were as to the future. If a girl was more than 18 or 19 years old and had borne none, it lessened her market value. Such perfectly natural and even inevitable incidents of slave-trading were often regarded by travelers as outrageous. Charles R. Weld, an English barrister, illustrates this in describing what he saw: 'Personal examination [of the women in public] was confined to the hands, arms, legs, bust and teeth. Searching questions were put respecting their age and whether they had [had] children. If they replied in the negative, their bosoms were generally handled in a repulsive and disgusting manner.' A matter-of-fact New Yorker recorded his impressions as follows:—'In those days, all frocks were secured in the back with hooks and eyes, so that it was an easy matter to go to the women and unhook their dresses and examine their backs for any signs of flogging. In fact such signs made a woman unsalable. As all purchases were warranted, if any trader, after a sale, was suspicious of a diseased condition, he took the woman upstairs into a private room where she was subjected to a physical examination.'"[80] Further, female slaves, even when not up on sale, were at any and all times and on

---

[80] F. Bancroft, op. cit., p. 108. See also Dr. J. Welzl, op. cit., pp. 79-80, for further details of the intimate examination of female slaves by prospective purchasers.

any or no provocation liable to a most personal physical scrutiny by any man in power over them who chose to exercise his right,—master, overseer, jailer, or the like.[81]

Examples of such aspects of slave-trading are always revolting and inhuman and frequently they are pathetic as well, as in the following instance occurring in a great slave sale of over four hundred Negroes that took place in Savannah in March, 1859:

"The family of Primus, plantation carpenter, consisting of Daphney his wife, with her young babe, and Dido, a girl of three years old, were reached in due course of time. Daphney had a large shawl, which she kept carefully wrapped around her infant and herself. This unusual proceeding attracted much attention, and provoked many remarks, such as these:

" 'What do you keep your nigger covered up for? Pull off her blanket.'

" 'What's the matter with the gal? Has she got the headache?'

" 'What's the fault of the gal? Ain't she sound? Pull off her rags and let us see her.'

" 'Who's going to bid on that nigger, if you keep her covered up. Let's see her face.' * * *

"At last the auctioneer obtained a hearing long enough to explain that there was no attempt to practise any deception in the case—the parties were not to be wronged in any way; he had no desire to palm off on them an inferior article; but the truth of the matter was that

---

[81] Dr. J. Welzl, *op. cit.,* pp. 82-84.

Daphney had been confined only fifty days ago, and he thought that on that account she was entitled to the slight indulgence of a blanket, to keep from herself and child the chill air and the driving rain."[82]

A further evidence of the minute, inconsiderate bodily examination to which Negresses were at all times open can be found in the wording and details of the advertisements published by masters of runaway female slaves in which the most intimate and personal of marks or blemishes are described, thus demonstrating that not only were the masters familiar with the contours of their female slaves, from head to toe, but also that any one apprehending such fugitive Negresses would experience no least hesitation in putting them through the most thorough investigation in an attempt to discover any such tell-tale marks.[83]

Finally, before passing on to a more detailed treatment of the major aspects of sexual slavery in the old South, let us merely mention the opportunity for sadistic indulgence on the part of the master class in the frequent and brutally excessive floggings practised on the Negro slaves, as well as in a multitude of various other cruel humiliations and tortures. As this feature of the situation is somewhat remote from our central theme, we shall pass it by here, particularly as information on it abounds in the majority of works treating of slavery.

[82] F. Bancroft, op. cit., pp. 231-232.
[83] See Dr. J. Welzl, op. cit., p. 82, for examples of such advertisements.

2. Marriage among Slaves

To speak of marriage among our Negro slaves is the same as to speak of honor among thieves, for both refer to conditions existing, or being allowed to exist, only when there was no good, or poor, reason against it and when nothing was lost by it. If two slaves wished to marry and the master saw nothing in the union in any way to affect his income from their labor, he would likely give his consent to it. However, if in his eyes there was any circumstance which militated against the advisability of the pairing, he would forbid it, and the slaves had no smallest possibility of marrying, so absolute was his control over them and their movements. Further, if he had permitted them to join in wedlock and then for any, or no, motive regretted it, he could annul the marriage; or if the consortium proved infertile he could compel the woman to take a different mate, or several mates; in short, he could order their "marital" life as he saw fit. "Life [among the slaves] was without doubt monogamous in general; and some of the matings were by order, though the generality were pretty surely spontaneous."[84] Slave marriages were merely tolerated, and they were "subject to change without notice." "There were no legalized marriages for slaves, and the master had the power of separating families by sale or removal. Usually a ceremony was performed, sometimes by a white minister, more often by a Negro preacher. As the offspring fol-

[84] Ulrich B. Phillips, op. cit., p. 204.

lowed the condition of the mother, marrying off the plantation was discouraged, and many times forbidden. Telfair [a planter] prohibited marriages from taking place between the slaves on his several plantations." [85]

The complete lack of legality to these marriages is amply demonstrated by the fact of their annulment being entirely a matter of the will or whim of the master. "Slave marriages, not being legal contracts, might be dissolved without recourse to public tribunals. Only the master's consent was required, and this was doubtless not hard to get. On one plantation systematic provision was made in the standing regulations: 'When sufficient cause can be shewn on either side, a marriage may be annulled; but the offending party must be severely punished. Where both are in the wrong, both must be punished, and if they insist on separating must have a hundred lashes apiece. After such a separation, neither can marry again for three years.'... But it may be presumed that most plantation rules were not so stringent." [86] Slave marriage just did not appear important to the master class; one might as well be serious over the matings of his cattle. Moreover, sanction of a binding marriage would seriously have disturbed the rights of ownership. "Neither marriage nor fatherhood among slaves was legally recognized because recognition would have gravely interfered with property rights; and the legal prohibitions against dividing families were very slight. Whatever

[85] R. B. Flanders, *op. cit.*, pp. 172-173.
[86] Ulrich B. Phillips, *op. cit.*, p. 205.

recognition family relations received was, with few exceptions, voluntary."[87]

Maternity of a child was important, for the owner of the mother was the owner of the offspring; but marriage and paternity were left pretty well to shift for themselves. It is quite likely that at some places there was even "an actual sanction of polygamy by some of the masters. A planter doubtless described a practise not unique when he said 'that he interfered as little as possible with their domestic habits except in matters of police. "We don't care what they do when their tasks are over—we lose sight of them till next day. Their morals and manners are in their own keeping. The men may have, for instance, as many wives as they please, so long as they do not quarrel about such matters."'"[88] This attitude is virtually identical with that found by Olmsted, as reported by another writer:[89]

"When inspecting a large plantation in the lower Miss. valley, Olmsted asked if the Negroes began to have children at a very early age. '"Sometimes at sixteen," said the manager. "Yes, and at fourteen," said the overseer * * *. Women were almost common property, though sometimes the men were not at all inclined to acknowledge it; for when I asked: "Do you not try to discourage this?" the overseer answered: "No, not unless they quarrel." "They get jealous and quarrel among themselves sometimes about it," the manager explained,

[87] F. Bancroft, *op. cit.,* p. 197.
[88] Ulrich B. Phillips, *op. cit.,* p. 204.
[89] F. Bancroft, *op. cit.,* p. 85, note 42.

"or come to the overseer and complain, and he has them punished." "Give all hands a damned good hiding," said the overseer. You punish for adultery, then, but not for fornication? "Yes," answered the manager, but "No," insisted the overseer, "we punish them for quarreling; if they don't quarrel I don't mind anything about it, but if it makes a muss, I give all four of 'em a warning."'"

Nevertheless, though marriage and paternity among the slaves were rather irrelevant in the eyes of the masters, still they often favored some sort of regular, settled mating among their Negroes and would at times even offer some inducements to that end; but this was done largely in the interest of order on the plantation and health and contentment among the slaves, and rarely, if ever, sprang from moral grounds. "In perhaps a large majority of cases it was needless or futile to give attention to the paternity of the children. But on well-conducted plantations, matings—it was misleading to call them marriages when in law there was no such thing—were always favored, usually encouraged and sometimes virtually compelled, because believed to be conducive to order, health and industry as well as to natural increase. Every planter preferred the matings to be between his own slaves, when numbers and ages were suitable, and it was not rare for a large planter to make it a positive restriction...James H. Hammond of South Carolina gave an additional bounty of $5 to first 'marriages,' and doubtless many others offered special inducements. After that, if the pickaninnies were numerous at the quarters, and there were no violent jealousies, no disturbances of the peace, little or no attention was given to the paternity of the children. It was, of course, different with the servants at the 'big house,' where ostensible decencies were attempted to be maintained for the sake of the master's family." [90]

All this rigorous control of and absolute power over the sexual affairs of the slaves, even in those affairs which were personally rather remote from the master, is indicative of the most abject sort of sexual slavery among the Negroes of our old South.

3. Overseers and Slaves

Othello, in giving vent to his bitter exclamation:

> "O curse of marriage,
> That we can call these delicate creatures ours,
> And not their appetites!"

by substituting *planting* for *marriage,* might well have voiced the sentiments of absentee planters concerning their overseers, although they probably would also have wished to replace *delicate* with *damned*. These men, in complete power and not checked by the presence of the owner nor hindered by the responsibility of ownership, being merely paid employees, were constantly guilty of taking advantage of their position and of committing excesses and abuses against those under them. In the great majority of cases they seem ever to have been a burden and source of worry and aggravation to their employers, to say nothing of to the slaves.

[90] *Ibid.,* pp. 84-85.

Naturally, planters were continually trying new overseers in the hope of finding a satisfactory one, and rarely
succeeding. "James Tait [an Alabama planter] seems to
have changed his overseers nearly every year. One in
1837 was particularly annoying. Among his offenses
were a failure to tan leather, though he pretended to
have done it; neglecting a fire in the field and permitting a fence to burn; neglecting live stock and slaves,
with consequent deaths of two horses, a mule, a steer, a
slave woman and a boy; letting the Negroes get fence
rails from a neighbor's woods and otherwise embroiling
Tait with adjacent planters; and 'making my negro men
run away by interfering with their wives, or on account
of the women.' These experiences prompted him to jot
maxims, never to talk to an overseer about his neighbors,
and with special emphasis: 'A legacy to my children.—
Never employ an overseer who will equalize himself
with the Negro women. Besides the morality of it, there
are evils too numerous to be now mentioned.'" [91]

Concubinage between the overseers and female slaves
could hardly have escaped being fairly common; the
coarse, brutal character of the men, their complete jurisdiction over the Negresses, and the general inaccessibility
of white women of any sort, all combined to make such
a result inevitable. Evidence of such cohabitations abound
in the records; even the more dependable type of overseer was not exempt. "In the middle 'fifties the overseer
on Chemonie [a Florida plantation of George Noble
Jones] was John Evans who though he begot two mulatto

[91] Ulrich B. Phillips, *op. cit.*, pp. 281-282.

children before he took a wife, was trustworthy, sagacious
and steady-going." [92] When Evans was taken to task for
this by his employer, he quit Jones' service,[93] evidently
feeling that such conduct was his inalienable right as an
overseer. It seems to have been taken more or less for
granted that an overseer, especially if he was single,
would misconduct himself with the Negresses under him.
"The conduct of J. W. Ledbetter, one of Carter's [a large
planter] overseers, led him to write his employer that he
was confident that 'there has been Tails and Lies tole
on me till I am getting tired of them,' and called forth a
long but rather unconvincing defense of his conduct with
one of the female slaves. He stoutly averred that never
'have I ever had any intercoarse with hear in my life.'. .
Just how prevalent was concubinage it is impossible to
say; certainly it was not unknown. An absolute master
on a plantation the owner of which was far removed, and
having full control over the bodies of the female slaves,
it would be rather difficult for an ignorant, intemperate,
and morally weak individual not to take advantage of his
position. Even owners themselves were subject to liaisons
with attractive mulatto slaves." [94]

Naturally, the planters' prayer was ever for a steady,
dependable overseer who was not greatly given to licentiousness; a prayer which was seldom answered. Various
planters have left rather elaborate descriptions of and
specifications for the ideal overseer. "They asked of the

[92] *Ibid.*, p. 269.
[93] R. B. Flanders, *op. cit.*, p. 142.
[94] *Ibid.*, pp. 141-142.

overseer as constant attendance as possible with the gangs in the fields by day and at the stables night and morning; and they deprecated severity and forbade indecency in the infliction of punishment. One of these included among his rules: 'Having connection 'with any of my female servants will most certainly be visited with a dismissal from my employment, and no excuses can or will be taken.' Another proprietor [of Mississippi],...who surely had no written rules, related in a letter to his nephew and niece in North Carolina: 'I turned away my overseer this morning about Harriot and my house girl, for they both say they are big to him. I think if they are I shall pay them for their gallantry. I caut him and my gals abed together last night.' " [95] It seems in general that absentee proprietors were most insistent on strict morality in their overseers, probably because they felt that such morality might induce a kindred conscientiousness in the discharge of their other duties and a better conducted and more profitable plantation; but when they were resident they frequently were not such moral sticklers, particularly as concerned themselves. But be all this as it may, a South Carolinian seems to have summed up the requirements for ideal overseers when he advertised in the *South Carolina Gazette,* January 6, 1787, for two who had to be "capable, sober and not passionate." [96]

[95] Ulrich B. Phillips, *op. cit.,* p. 323.
[96] *Ibid.,* p. 323.

4. *Concubinage: Masters and Slaves*

The matter of sexual relations between the master class and the slaves of the old South is strikingly typical of so many of America's social problems; the greater its magnitude, the greater the attempt made to suppress recognition of even the existence of the situation. Any one with any knowledge of human nature and its workings under the stimulus of power could readily, even knowing nothing of the actual conditions, arrive at a fair picture of things as they were under Negro slavery. Apologists for slavery, naturally, and determined renovators of American morality have frequently tried most courageously to disprove the existence of concubinage in the South to any important degree, or have even denied it altogether, limiting it to mere isolated instances at the hands of "depraved persons" who would be guilty of misconduct in any society in which they might find themselves. However, such a position can be maintained only by closing the eyes to a wealth of quite obvious facts. "This form of sex relation [concubinage] was fairly common in certain sections during the period of slavery... To what extent the relationship existed during slavery days or even at the present time, it is not possible to say. The custom varied in different sections and in the same section at different times. No doubt there were isolated instances of the sort everywhere, throughout the whole period that the Negro has been in the country. That it was a uniform custom of the slave-owning class, there is no reason to believe: that it was common in certain regions, there is no reason to doubt." [97] And this, I feel, is the fairest and most lenient view of the matter that can be taken, and it explains certain individuals who dogmatically deny that concubinage had any place in the South, by supposing that these persons hailed from those sections of the country where it happened not to be prevalent.

But proof of intimacy between masters and slaves is in nowise lacking. For one thing, even today a large part of the white men of any means in the average medium-size Southern town support a Negro or mulatto mistress, although often they are married to white women.[98] Such a situation under emancipation is indicative of what was to be expected in slavery times. Bancroft asserts that: "Inter-race sexual immorality was one of the worst features of slavery. A Southern judge and ex-Confederate soldier wrote to the author that 'the moral results of slavery, in its most favorable aspects, are unprintable.'"[99]

But even more unequivocal proof is to be had in the mulatto. "Actual race mixture is proven by the presence in the South of two million mulattoes; it is no new thing, for it has been going on steadily ever since the African appeared in the United States, though there are people who insist there was little or no amalgamation until Northern soldiers came down during the war and re-

[97] Edward B. Reuter, *The Mulatto in the United States,* Boston, 1918, pp. 139-140.
[98] For some well authenticated instances of recent occurrence (1910), see A. B. Hart, *The Southern South,* N. Y., 1910, pp. 153ff.
[99] F. Bancroft, *op. cit.,* p. 328.

mained in garrison during Reconstruction. Every intelligent traveller in the ante-bellum period, every candid observer, is a witness to the contrary. Since the earliest settlements there have continually been, and still exist, two different forms of illicit relations between the sexes—concubinage and general irregularity. Whence came the hundreds of thousands of mulattoes in slavery days? Of course the child of a mulatto will be normally light, and of the two million mulattoes now in the country, very likely three-fourths are children of mulattoes. But what are the other five hundred thousand?"[100] On all sides we find testimony to support the frequent cohabitation of whites and slaves. "Concubinage of Negro women to planters and their sons and overseers is evidenced by the census enumeration of mulattoes and other data.[101] It was flagrantly prevalent in the Creole section of Louisiana, and was at least sporadic from New England to Texas. The régime of slavery facilitated concubinage not merely by making black women subject to white men's wills but by promoting intimacy and weakening racial antipathy."[102]

These mulattoes, the offspring of mulatto and slave, seem on the whole to have been the recipients of no great amount of consideration from the master simply because

[100] A. B. Hart, *op. cit.*, p. 152.
[101] It is hinted, for example, by the exclamation point in this Virginian letter of 1831: "P. P. Burton has quit his wife, sent her to her father's and gone off with Sandy Burton to Texas and taken a female slave along!" [Note of Phillips.]
[102] Ulrich B. Phillips, *op. cit.*, p. 205.

he was their father. "Most frequently their children fared just as any other slaves; but not always. Such incidents as these, however, but emphasize the evil effects of slavery on both the dominant and subject race."[103] Of course, there were instances in which the masters provided adequately in their wills for their mulatto children, and even for their Negro mistresses, but these were exceptions to the generality of cases.

It would be indeed comforting for the vanity of the white race if it could truthfully be maintained that the sexual irregularity in the old South sprang largely from the Negro, a product of his general licentiousness and moral laxness, and that the white man was something of a victim of circumstances in the matter. But unfortunately such was not the fact. "In summarizing, we may say that the intermixture of the races everywhere has gone on to the extent of the white man's wishes. The Negro woman never has objected to, and has generally courted, the relationship. It was never at any time a matter of compulsion; on the contrary it was a matter of being honored by a man of a superior race. Speaking generally, the amount of intermixture is limited only by the self-respect of the white man and the compelling strength of the community sentiment."[104]

However, despite Reuter's view of the matter, it is more than likely that the acquiescence of the slaves to the white man's lust, while doubtless often freely granted, was not so entirely free of coercion as he would

[103] B. G. Brawley, *op. cit.,* pp. 57-58.
[104] E. B. Reuter, *op. cit.,* pp. 162-163.

have us believe. Compulsion can be brought to bear in many other and far more subtle ways than through brute force, and a slave-master was certainly in a position to bring any and all pressure to bear on his Negresses if necessary. Says a German authority: "In particular the weak woman was subject to the unbridled passion of the slave owner; moreover, if the slave woman had a good figure and a pleasing appearance she was subject to the insane jealousy of her white mistress without any protection. This whole matter belongs to the darkest chapters of American Negro slavery." [105]

On the whole, it is probable that this concubinage was rather an orderly business, as such matters go, everything considered. "In general, it seems not to have been a promiscuous relation between the master class and the female slaves, but a relation between some favorite slave girl and a young man of the family." [106] Naturally, that is to say that the relationship was not ordinarily promiscuous at any one time, but it does not imply that a master might not from time to time change mistresses from among his slaves.

But generalities, though very enlightening, are rarely overly convincing; therefore, to mend this lack it may not be amiss to cite a few examples in point. One of our best sources for such data is law cases of the slavery era, and in particular divorce cases, as the following one from Tennessee:

"Richmond v. Richmond, 10 Yerger 343, December

[105] Dr. J. Welzl, *op. cit.*, p. 79.
[106] E. B. Reuter, *op. cit.*, p. 140.

1837. Petition for a divorce . . . 'adultery . . . with the negro Polly, . . . took . . . Polly . . . to keep house for him . . . in the habit of sitting by the fire with Polly after the laborers in the shop had gone to bed.' Evidence of his relations with her . . . 'tried by a jury, and the issue found against the defendant.' Decree affirmed." [107]

An equally, if not more, fertile source of evidence for Negro concubinage in the old South is to be found in the executions of some of the planters' wills, in which they often openly acknowledged their Negro mistresses and mulatto children and made some provision for them, as, for example, in these two instances from South Carolina:

"Fable v. Brown, 2 Hill Eq. 378, March 1835. 'John Fable, a foreigner, settled in Charleston some years ago, . . . He had two [illegitimate] colored children by a female slave . . . executed . . . will . . . 1831 . . . "The residue of my property I will and bequeath to my children, whom I acknowledge, to be divided share and share alike . . ." ' " [108]

"Farr vs. Thompson, Executor of Farr, Cheves 37, Fall 1839 . . . 'the testator was never married. He had lived for many years in a state of illicit intercourse with a [bright] mulatto woman, his own slave ["the child of . . . a half brother of testator"] who assumed the position of a wife, and controlled, at least, all the domestic arrangements of the family.' " [109]

Possibly one of the most famous, or rather notorious, cases of concubinage in the old days was that of David

[107] H. T. Catterall, op. cit., vol. II, p. 505.
[108] Ibid., p. 357.
[109] Ibid., p. 375.

Dickson, of Georgia, who "was as unusual in his marital relations as he was successful in the planting industry. According to one of his close friends, while a young man he became attached to a mulatto girl, about his age, who was a waiting maid in his father's house. Falling heir to this slave upon the death of his father, Dickson lived with her as man with wife, becoming the father of several mulatto children. So open was Dickson in this respect that he was banned from polite society. Upon his death in 1885 he left his entire estate, some half million dollars, to his concubine, who bore his name, Amanda A. Dickson." [110]

These Negro concubines were sometimes the objects of apparently very real and strong attachments on the part of their masters; nothing else could have compelled the white man to endure the adverse public sentiment and frequently humiliating circumstances of his liaison. Such records as the following impress us with the patent intensity of the man's passion: "About 1846 Elijah Willis of South Carolina, unmarried, 'began to live in concubinage with one of his female slaves,... Amy, who bore [him] five mulatto children... two of them died;... Amy ["a dark yellow woman"] was not handsome... had several husbands before she took up with Willis... Amy's last husband is still on Willis' plantation;... Willis was distressed when one of the children died.'" [111]

However, these records attest to not only the master's ardor for his concubine but frequently they also bear

[110] R. B. Flanders, *op. cit.*, pp. 271-272.
[111] H. T. Catterall, *op. cit.*, vol. II, p. 469.

witness to his brutality and cruel callousness by the manner in which he conducted himself with her in respect to his white wife and the various indignities he made the latter suffer. This divorce suit from South Carolina gives a fair picture of such a situation:

"Jelineau vs. Jelineau, 2 Desaussure 45, June 1801 ... 'bill ... for alimony ... that the complainant, [a lady from St. Domingo] intermarried in ... February, 1800, with Francis Jelineau, (also from St. Domingo) ... That he cohabited with his own slave, by whom he had a mulatto child, on whom he lavished his affection; whilst he daily insulted the complainant, and encouraged his slave to do the same ... That at dinner one day, he took away the plate from complainant when she was going to help herself to something to eat, and said, when he and the negro had dined she might.' 'The defendant states that at the time he was about to marry the complainant, he informed her that he had a mulatto child, born to him in St. Domingo, [where he stated, it was not disgraceful to have such connexions] ... and the complainant promised to behave kindly to said child.' Alimony decreed." [112]

But an even more extraordinary arrangement occurred in North Carolina:

"Hausley vs. Hausley, 10 Iredell 506, December 1849. 'A suit ... for a divorce a vinculo matrimonii ... and for alimony ... "her husband not only abandoned her bed entirely, and bedded with ... Negro Lucy, but he deprived the petitioner of the control of all those domestic duties ... which belong to a wife, and placed ... Lucy in

[112] *Ibid.,* p. 281.

the full possession...and insulted the petitioner by... repeatedly ordering her to give place to the...negro, and saying that the petitioner was an encumbrance, and encouraged...Lucy to treat her also;...that often he would, at night, compel the petitioner to sleep in bed with...Lucy, when he would treat...Lucy as his wife, he occupying the same bed with the petitioner and... Lucy...that she at length, abandoned the residence of her husband." ' " [113]

Perhaps it would be wise, and no more than fair, to pause for a moment at this point to warn the reader against the danger of getting an entirely disproportionate view of the matter in hand. This chapter is devoted to the study of the sexual aspects of slavery and consequently all the data in it is especially selected to that end; but let no one conclude from the preponderance of erotic material here presented that American Negro slavery was one long orgy and wild debauch. Such a picture of things would be as distorted as that commonly presented by slavery sympathizers who hold up the old plantation as just one "big happy family" on which the Negro was "better off" than he is under freedom. Abuse and lustful indulgence there was in plenty, as we have seen, but on the whole it was secondary, an inescapable concomitant to slavery. Let no one suppose that the trade in "likely Negro wenches" went on apace solely to minister to the sensual appetites of the masters. As Phillips puts it, in speaking of the qualifications that readily sold slaves: "Demonstrable talents in artisanry would of course en-

[113] *Ibid.*, p. 139.

hance a man's value; and unusual good looks on the part of a young woman might stimulate the bidding of men interested in concubinage." [114] But even so, in the average run of such cases the purchase of young, handsome Negresses was not often made solely for carnal reasons; she had still to be a slave and earn her bread, her evenings leaving her ample time to discharge her concubinary duties. Phillips himself believes that purchase for mere concubinage was rare, and goes on to say: "Among the thousands of bills of sale which the present writer has scanned, in every quarter of the South, many have borne record of exceptional prices for men, mostly artisans and 'drivers'; but the few women who brought unusually high prices were described in virtually every case as fine seamstresses, parlor maids, laundresses, hotel cooks, and the like. Another indication against the multiplicity of purchases for concubinage is that the great majority of the women listed in these records were bought in family groups. Concubinage itself was fairly frequent, particularly in southern Louisiana; but no frequency of purchases for it as a predominant purpose can be demonstrated from authentic records." [115] However, all this is not to say that there was not an undeniable traffic in black female flesh for lustful purposes, but merely that this business was relatively small as compared to the volume of trading in young female slaves in general. There was the whole matter of the "fancy girl" trade, which we shall now examine a bit.

[114] U. B. Phillips, *American Negro Slavery*, N. Y., 1918, p. 193.
[115] *Ibid.*, p. 193.

The "fancy girl" was one of a class of young slave girls, sometimes Negro but usually mulatto, of good figure and pleasing, or often even beautiful, appearance, such as would serve to feed the flames of her owner's lusts and offer ample opportunity for their satisfaction. These girls, though at times required to act also as servants for their masters, were nevertheless bought with the idea of their carnal possibilities uppermost in their purchaser's mind, and were in fact displayed to this end by the trader and priced accordingly, some of them fetching amazing sums. "In small numbers and of varying complexions they were to be seen in nearly all Southern markets. Traders gladly exhibited them and were proud of the high prices they commanded; visitors were curious to see them and sure to tell about them later. Miss Bremer wrote of some in Richmond: 'In another "jail" were kept the so-called "fancy girls" for fancy purchasers. They were handsome fair mulattoes, some of them almost white girls.' Her comment on those seen in Augusta, Georgia, was: 'Many of these children [from 12 to 20 years of age] were fair mulattoes, and some of them very pretty. One girl of twelve was so white, that I would have supposed her to belong to the white race; her features, too, were those of the whites. The slave-keeper told us that the day before, another girl, still fairer and handsomer, had been sold for $1,500. These white children of slavery become, for the most part, victims of crime, and sink to the deepest degradation.' "[116]

The "fancy girls" were kept quite separate by the

[116] F. Bancroft, op. cit., pp. 328-329.

traders from mere female slaves, and though there was nothing ostentatious in it, they were commonly displayed in such a manner as to leave small doubt of the office they were intended to fill, and any last doubt that might have remained would have speedily been dispelled by their price. Orville H. Browning, Secretary of the Interior in Johnson's cabinet, in 1854 visited a slave jail in Lexington, Kentucky, and described what he saw: " 'In several of the rooms I found very handsome mulatto women, of fine persons and easy genteel manners, sitting at their needle-work awaiting a purchaser. The proprietor made them get up and turn around to show to advantage their finely developed and graceful forms.' $1,600 was the price of one of the girls.

"Do you wonder why the trader did not have them display their needle-work instead of their 'finely developed and graceful forms'? Obviously they were of the class everywhere known as 'fancy girls,' prospective concubines—common in all large markets, but rarely so advantageously displayed. Except New Orleans, Lexington was perhaps the best place in all the South to specialize in them; for it was a great center or a favorite resort for prosperous horse-breeders, reckless turfmen, spendthrift planters, gamblers and profligates, whose libertinism was without race prejudice." [117]

Gamblers, saloonkeepers, race-track men, and debauchees of all sorts, dreamed of owning a "fancy girl," not only for readily understandable personal reasons, but also as a valuable business asset. Naturally, the racing

[117] *Ibid.,* p. 131.

and gambling centers were likely to be the places at which trade in these girls most briskly flourished, and head and shoulders above all such localities stood New Orleans. "New Orleans—where thousands of sporting men and voluptuaries lived and other thousands came for the racing season, the Carnival and dissipation—was fully tenfold the largest market for 'fancy girls.' The prospect of great profit induced their conspicuous display. At the mart...a handsome quadroon girl, gayly dressed and adorned with ribbons and jewels, sat in a show-window to attract attention. 'She, too, was for sale, as a choice house-servant, at a high price on account of her beauty. As our friend the planter was about to leave the premises he glanced at this girl, and asked what the trader would take for her. Being told, he shook his head, leered at the slave, and said, with an oath, "Too expensive."' Charles Casey, an English traveler, saw 'a beautiful quadroon girl, neatly dressed and very intelligent,' sell for $2,000 in Evan's Arcade, in New Orleans, at a time when field hands brought from $600 to $800. And 'Ole Charley' Logan bought a bright mulatto girl, Violetta, for $600, in Columbia, South Carolina, took her to New Orleans in one of his coffles and sold her for $1,500."[118]

The exorbitant prices demanded by traders for these girls, and obtained from purchasers, so far in excess of the normal, current value of slaves, is possibly the most conclusive proof of the real purpose behind their barter. The values placed on them were often entirely out of

[118] *Ibid.*, pp. 329-330.

reason, that is out of all reason save the particular one for which the Southern gallants strove to gain possession of them. The Memphis *Eagle and Enquirer,* June 26, 1857, carried the following editorial item: "A slave woman is advertised to be sold in St. Louis who is so surpassingly beautiful that $5,000 has already been offered for her, at private sale, and refused." [119]

As has already been said, by far the largest market and trading center of "fancy girls" was New Orleans, and in that city the most important and elegant of such places of barter was the French exchange, in the rotunda of the St. Louis Hotel. This hotel was located in the old city; it covered almost an entire square and was bordered by St. Louis, Chartres, Toulouse, and Royal streets. Here, amidst the most luxurious surroundings, "superior looking girls, varying from mulatto to octoroon," were most often to be seen offered at auction. There came prosperous gamblers, successful turfmen, sedate and respectable planters, all to pander to their lusts in the greatest of comfort under the protecting guise of utilizing the economic institution of slavery.[120]

An interesting and rather curious variation of the traffic in "fancy girls" was their occasional being offered as the prize in a raffle. "Two English ladies, the Misses Turnbull, were much shocked in New Orleans by a handbill announcing a raffle for several things, in-

[119] *Ibid.,* p. 329.
[120] For further details of the old St. Louis Hotel and of the manner of conducting auctions of girls there, see F. Bancroft, *op. cit.,* pp. 333 ff.

cluding a mulatto seamstress and lady's maid, 18 years of age, together with a horse, wagon and other things. It was something to attract 'sports.' Success prompts repetition and imitation. 'The enterprising and go-ahead Colonel Jennings has got a raffle under way now, which eclipses all his previous undertakings in that line,' said the New Orleans *True Delta*. It was for 'the celebrated trotting horse "Star," buggy and harness' and a 'stout mulatto girl "Sarah," aged about twenty years, a general house servant.'" [121]

The esteem in which the masters held their colored concubines can be deduced from their attempts to recover them when they had run away. All the Southern newspapers of that period would frequently carry notices of offers of reward for the return to the master of his dusky darling. W. D. Smith of Williamsport, Louisiana, in the Sunday supplement of the *Picayune*, January 2, 1859, offered $100 for the recovery of Livinia, a mulattress of about 27 years of age, who had run away. "She is very intelligent and pretty good looking," ran the item. "She is remarkably well provided with clothes of fair quality, and had on when she left a white silk bonnet..." At this same time, A. Lauraine of 96 Canal St., New Orleans, offered a like sum for the return of his Elizabeth. "She is in color black...has a fine suit of hair, stands erect, speaks French and English well, and in appearance [is] handsome; weighs about 130 pounds." [122] Such advertisements were by no means a novelty.

[121] F. Bancroft, *op. cit.*, pp. 327-328.

[122] *Ibid.*, note, p. 329.

But the highest development of colored concubinage seems not to have been between slave and master, but between free mulatto women and non-slave-holding white men. This system obtained to a variable extent throughout the South, but in Charleston, Mobile, and particularly in New Orleans, it reached a stage which could very readily have been termed a "socially sanctioned institution." Olmsted describes this system so well that I quote him at some length.[123]

"I refer to a class composed of the illegitimate offspring of white men and colored women (mulattoes or quadroons), who, from the habits of early life, the advantages of education, and the use of wealth, are too much superior to the negroes, in general, to associate with them, and are not allowed by law, or the popular prejudice, to marry white people. The girls are frequently sent to Paris to be educated, and are very accomplished. They are generally pretty, and often handsome. I have rarely, if ever, met more beautiful women, than one or two of them, that I saw by chance, in the streets. They are much better formed, and have a much more graceful and elegant carriage than Americans in general...Their beauty and attractiveness being their fortune, they cultivate and cherish with diligence every charm or accomplishment they are possessed of.

"Of course, men are attracted by them, associate with them, are captivated, and become attached to them, and, not being able to marry them legally, and with the usual

[123] Olmsted, *A Journey in the Seaboard Slave States,* pp. 594-597, cited by E. B. Reuter, *op. cit.,* pp. 141-143.

forms and securities for constancy, make such arrangements 'as can be agreed upon.' When a man makes a
declaration of love to a girl of this class, she will admit or
deny, as the case may be, her happiness in receiving it;
but, supposing she is favorably disposed, she will usually
refer the applicant to her mother. The mother inquires,
like a Countess of Kew, into the circumstances of the
suitor; ascertains whether he is able to maintain a family, and, if satisfied with him, in these and other respects,
requires from him security that he will support her
daughter in a style suitable to what she has been bred
to, and that, if he should ever leave her, he will give her
a certain sum for her future support, and a certain additional sum for each of the children she shall then have.

"...Everything being satisfactorily arranged, a tenement in a certain quarter of the town is usually hired,
and the couple move into it and go to housekeeping—
living as if they were married....

"During all the time a man sustains this relation, he
will commonly be moving, also, in reputable society on
the other side of town; not improbably, eventually he
marries, and has a family establishment elsewhere. Before doing this, he may separate from his *placée* (so she
is termed). If so, he pays her according to agreement, and
as much more, perhaps, as his affection for her, or his
sense of the cruelty of the proceeding, may lead him to;
and she has the world before her again, in the position
of a widow. Many men continue, for a long time, to support both establishments—particularly, if their legal marriage is one *de convenance*."

In conclusion, there is one phase of white-Negro concubinage that we may briefly inspect before closing this section: the cohabitation of white women with male Negro slaves. As may readily be guessed, this was at best of mere sporadic occurrence throughout the South and never received any degree of the complaisance or tolerance of public opinion that was accorded to the system of concubinage of the masters and female slaves. Such women, on the whole, as indulged in this sort of libertinage were frowned upon and rejected by good society and, if married, their conduct generally led to divorce when discovered; records of such divorce suits give us most of our evidence in this connection. It is amusing to compare the great freedom that the white men permitted themselves with their Negresses, to the strict morality they demanded of their wives—a sort of concubinary "Double Standard,"—but this duality of sexual ethics has been present in human affairs since the beginning of time. But let us examine a few typical instances of such female irregularity.

North Carolina seems to have been a state in which color indiscrimination on the part of white women in choosing their bedfellows was particularly prevalent, for all the cases I cite below hail from that locality, as for example:

"Re Puckett, 2 Col. Rec. N. C. 704, July 1727. 'A presentment against Elizabeth Puckett for that she hath left her husband and hath for some years cohabited with a Negro man of Capt. Simon Jefferies.'"[124]

[124] H. T. Catterall, *op. cit.*, vol. II, p. 12.

In the following case, the woman appears to have been primarily interested in securing a male, and to have regarded his color as of secondary importance:

"Whittington vs. Whittington, 2 Dev. & Bat. 64. December 1836. Petition for a divorce stated 'that the defendant [after their separation] had indulged in criminal intercourse with both whites and mulattoes:...and that she had three illegitimate children, one of which was a coloured child.'"[125]

This next instance is remarkable as a striking example of understatement of a husband's reaction to obvious evidence of his wife's infidelity:

"Lamb vs. Pigford, 1 Jones Eq. 195, June 1854... 'the plaintiff, a man of weak intellect, illiterate and easily imposed on...had become much dissatisfied with the conduct of his wife, who had given birth to a colored child, left his domicil and went to live with his brother, ...he made an absolute conveyance of the...land he had been living on, also of his slaves, six in number,...to exclude his wife from sharing in the...property.'"[126]

The two succeeding cases are curious in that they exemplify the complexities of jurisprudence that often confronted the courts in such matters:

"Walters v. Jordan, 12 Iredell 170, June 1851... 'petition by a widow for a year's allowance out of the personal estate of her late husband, who died intestate...The intestate seduced the petitioner and lived in adultery with her and then married her. After the marriage and

[125] *Ibid.*, p. 76.
[126] *Ibid.*, p. 183.

while they were living together, the petitioner—she and her husband being white persons—had criminal conversation with a negro man, by whom she became pregnant. The husband ... ordered the petitioner to leave his house. She did so ... and by his permission lived in another house on his premises, where she was delivered of a mulatto child. The husband did not receive her into his family again, nor treat her as his wife, further than to allow her to live in the said house and to maintain her there until his death, which happened soon after the birth of the child.'

"Held: 'the petitioner was entitled to a year's support' ... 'she did not "go away and continue with her adulterer" whom, as far as appears, she never saw after her husband forced her to live separately from him.' " [127]

But, not content to have gained this advantage, a year later finds her back in court suing, despite her flagrant and freely admitted misconduct, for her dower rights:

"Walters v. Jordan, 13 Iredell 361, June 1852 ... 'a petition for dower, ... the husband and wife had been married and lived together several years, until about three or four months before the husband's death; ... a witness deposes, that, on the day of the separation, ... as he was going to the house, he met the plaintiff coming away in tears; ... the husband told him, that he had understood his wife was pregnant by a negro man, and he had driven the strumpet off, and she should never live with him again ... a few months after the separation, he filed a bill against her for a divorce for cause of adultery

[127] *Ibid.*, pp. 157-158.

with a certain negro ["slave"] by whom she became pregnant of a child, ... When the copy of the bill was served,
it was read to her by the witness, who asked her if it was
so, and she held up the child and said it would show for
itself; the witness ... thought it was a negro child, and
asked her if it were not; and she replied that she was not
the first white woman that negro had taken in—that,
when he first came about her, she hated him, but that,
after a while, she loved him better than anybody in the
world, and she thought he must have given her something; that the witness then said, he did not blame her
husband for what he had done; and she replied, she did
not blame him for anything, except that he drove her off,
before he knew whether it would be a black child or not;
and the witness remarked that she (*sic*) supposed he had
good reasons to believe it ... evidence was also given,
tending to show, as it seemed to the Court, that, after
the separation, the plaintiff committed adultery with a
negro man ... though he is not identified to be the same
one, ... she continued apart from her husband, without
any reconciliation, until his death, and since that time
has been a lewd woman.' " [128]

However, sexual commerce between white women and
Negro men is no feature exclusively, or even of partial
necessity, of slavery; hence we shall pursue it no farther.
As far back as we know, white women of a sort have desired Negro men, and at the present day this type of
female is not scarce: Desdemona married a blackamoor,
and many French women are delighted at the privilege

[128] *Ibid.*, pp. 167-168.

of appearing in public in company with a robust darky. The racial characteristic of the rather notable preponderance in size of the black genitalia over that of the white is often given as one of the chief motivating factors in this situation, and this, coupled with the presence of a fiery, animal-like ardor and abandon, possibly explains a large part of such instances.

5. Slave-Breeding

What, to the present-day temper, will probably appear as the most revolting aspect of the sexual slavery of the Negroes of the old South, is the institution of slave-breeding, the deliberate prompting, or even forcing, on the part of the masters of the slaves to their prolific propagation so as to enable their owners to reap a profit from the crop of little pickaninnies, who would be sold as slaves when opportunity and their growth permitted it.

Such a proceeding represents, to my mind, the extremest phase and most subtle refinement of sexual slavery: when the issue of one's body, the fruits of one's love and intimacy with one's mate, can be and is stripped from one without recourse of any sort, disposed of quite without reference to the parents' will or desire, and when the production of this progeny is planned, guided, prompted, and even forced by another—that is sexual subjection indeed.

The whole business of slave-breeding, naturally, was dependent on the fact that the law and custom of the land gave the proprietor of the slave parents, more especially of the female parent, ownership of the offspring, just as in the case of other livestock.[129] But as the parentage of such children could be so complex and varied —being able to be born of two slave parents, owned by the same master or by different ones, of a free mother and slave father, or of a slave mother and a free father,— definite legislation was soon passed to fix the condition of the slave young. "By the time it had become generally enacted or understood in the colonies that a child born of slave parents should serve for life, a new question had arisen, that of the issue of a free person and a slave. This led Virginia in 1662 to lead the way with an act to the effect that the status of a child should be determined by that of the mother, which act both gave to slavery the sanction of law and made it hereditary."[130] Thus, as is true, so far as I know, the world over where slavery exists or has existed, the child of a female slave became a slave and was the property of the owner of its mother.

As is quite to be expected, such a shameful institution as slave-breeding is bound to find men to deny its existence, which denials constitute some of the strongest testimony for the repellency of the practise. For example, we find one such opinion: "It has been said by various anti-slavery spokesmen that many slaveowners systematically bred slaves for the market. They have adduced no shred of supporting evidence however; and although the present writer has long been alert for such data he has found but a single concrete item in the premises."[131]

[129] Ulrich B. Phillips, *Life and Labor in the Old South,* p. 162.
[130] B. G. Brawley, *op. cit.,* pp. 18-19.
[131] U. B. Phillips, *American Negro Slavery,* p. 361. (Throughout,

But, despite Mr. Phillips' conviction to the contrary, evidence of the practise, and extensive practise, of slave-breeding is quite ample. Prominent men of the day were profuse in their denunciations of the business. "The exportation [of slaves to other Southern States, said Thomas Jefferson Randolph] has averaged 8,500 for the last twenty years.... It is a practise, and an increasing practise in parts of Virginia, to rear slaves for market. How can an honorable mind, a patriot, and a lover of his country, bear to see this ancient dominion, rendered illustrious by the noble devotion and patriotism of her sons in the cause of liberty, converted into one grand menagerie where men are to be reared for market like oxen for the shambles.[?]" [132] However, as has ever been the case, and is preëminently so at the present time, the convictions expressed publicly by the great did not always represent their true feelings on the matter. "Ex-President Madison, who impressed even Harriet Martineau as having a profound hatred of slavery, commented on the licentiousness of the negroes, which he said, stopped short of only the destruction of the race, every slave girl being expected to be a mother by the time she was fifteen. Yet he could not conceal his pride in the fact that the latest count showed that one-third of his slaves were under five years of age—somewhat remote from race-suicide! This natural increase was always put on the

this book is very sympathetic toward and apologetic of American Negro slavery.)

[132] F. Bancroft, *op. cit.*, pp. 69-70.

profit side of the ledger, no matter how much the master complained of being impoverished by it." [133]

The possibility of profit from slave-breeding was a development of the later days of slavery. "For a long time it cost as much to raise a slave as he would ultimately be worth, and it was commonly thought to be cheaper to buy slaves than to rear them. The legal abolition of the slave trade, however, coinciding with the heavy demands imposed by the Louisiana Purchase and the development of the lower South, greatly changed matters. The slave increased in value, and Virginia and Maryland became famous breeding places for the plantations of the far South, a woman who was an extraordinary breeder being advertised as such. In 1832 the apologist for slavery wrote [Dew, in the *Pro-Slavery Argument*, p. 359]: 'Virginia is, in fact, a *negro* raising state for other states; she produces enough for her own supply, and six thousand for sale.' 'For the ten years preceding 1860 the average annual importation of slaves into the seven Southern states from the slave-breeding states was little less than twenty-five thousand.' [Olmsted, *The Cotton Kingdom*, I, 58.] On remote plantations the operation of the system was most gross; and a woman separated from her husband was forced to accept a new mate." [134]

"The prohibition of the African slave-trade after 1807 limited the future supply of slaves in the United States to virtually the natural increase. When the marvelous expansion of cotton culture caused an insatiable demand

[133] *Ibid.*, p. 74.
[134] B. G. Brawley, *op. cit.*, pp. 53-54.

for slaves, the need and profit of slave-rearing were obvious and inevitable." [185] Thus, whereas in the early days of American slavery the sale-price of a slave child would scarcely, if at all, recompense a slave owner for the loss of time and labor of the mother during childbirth and the rearing of the child plus the expense of his maintenance, in later years far greater profit could be drawn from breeding slaves than from working them. Prudent men would invest their capital in good breeding slaves as a safe, sure, and profitable source of income for their family, much as men of today invest it in stocks and bonds for the same purpose. In many localities slavery would have died out entirely of its own accord as unprofitable had it not been for its breeding aspects. Henry Clay declared that "nowhere in the farming portion of the United States would slave labor be generally employed, if the proprietor were not tempted to raise slaves by the high price of the Southern market, which keeps it [the price] up in his own." [186] Jesse Burton Harrison pointed out: "The only form in which it can safely be said that slaves on a plantation are profitable in Virginia, is in the multiplication of their number by births. If the proprietor, beginning with a certain number of negroes, can keep them for a few years from the hands of the sheriff or the slave trader, though their labour may have yielded him not a farthing of nett revenue, he finds that gradually but surely, his capital stock of negroes multiplies itself, and yields, if nothing else, a palpable interest

[185] F. Bancroft, *op. cit.*, p. 67.
[186] *Ibid.*, p. 69.

of young negroes." [187] In some states slaves were raised specifically for sale with no least thought of working them for their labor. Moncure D. Conway, the son of a slave-holder living near Fredericksburg, Virginia, wrote: "As a general thing, the chief pecuniary resource in the border States is the breeding of slaves; and I grieve to say that there is too much ground for the charges that general licentiousness among the slaves, for the purpose of a large increase, is compelled by some masters and encouraged by many. The period of maternity is hastened, the average youth of negro mothers being nearly three years earlier than that of any free race, and an old maid is utterly unknown among the women." [138]

All this, naturally, changed the aspect of things from what it had been in earlier years: whereas in the days when the labor of a slave was of prime importance and a breeding slave woman was regarded by the master as something of a liability because of the loss and expense to him, under the altered situation a prolific breeder was not only sought after by purchasers but also commanded a greater price. "A young female slave, unless skilled or comely, was, as Olmsted said, most prized for breeding qualities, and he quoted a Virginia planter who was proud of the fact that 'his women were uncommonly good breeders; he did not suppose that there was a lot of women anywhere that bred faster than his; he never heard of babies coming so fast as they did on his plantation; it was perfectly surprising; and every one of them,

[187] *Ibid.,* p. 72.
[138] *Ibid.,* pp. 76-77.

in his estimation, was worth two hundred dollars, as negroes were selling now, the moment it drew breath.'
Fecundity at an early age was considered a great virtue, and actual or prospective infants increased the market value of slave mothers.

"A girl of seventeen years that had borne two children was called a 'rattlin' good breeder' and commanded an extraordinary price.

"Young mothers with several small children were extremely valuable, and buxom girls of from 14 to 18 years were usually at a great premium because of good looks or proved or expected fecundity." [139]

It may be illuminating as to the value placed on fruitfulness by slave owners, to examine the wording of a few representative advertisements of the period in which the breeding qualities of Negroes offered for sale are extolled. One such advertisement of 1796, coming from Charleston, South Carolina, offers fifty especially fine Negroes for sale, and stresses the fact that they "are prime, their present Owner, with great trouble and expense, selected them out of many for several years past. They were purchased for stock and breeding Negroes, and to any Planter who particularly wanted them for that purpose, they are a very choice and desirable gang." [140] So well established and generally accepted was this practise that it was quite openly and freely recognized and countenanced. Southern newspapers of unquestioned high standing and long founded respectabil-

[139] *Ibid.,* pp. 81-83.
[140] *Ibid.,* p. 68.

ity quite readily accepted advertisements of this sort, as witness the following which appeared in the May 16, 1838, issue of the sedate Charleston *Mercury:*

"A GIRL about twenty years of age, raised in Virginia, and her two female children, one 4 and the other two years old. She is... remarkably strong and healthy, never having had a day's sickness, with the exception of the small pox, in her life. The children are fine and healthy. She is very prolific in her generating qualities, and affords a rare opportunity for any person who wishes to raise a family of strong and healthy servants for their own use. Sold for no fault." [141]

The Memphis *Avalanche,* February 25, 1860, strongly suggests present-day sales methods in its item:

"FANNY MUST GO!—SHE is a No. 1 girl, 18 years old, good house servant and hard to beat. Don't forget the *day,* such girls will *pay,* Saturday 25th, at 10 o'clock...— M. C. CAYCE & SON." [142]

And in New Orleans, an auctioneer, when selling a young female slave and her baby, lauded his offering thusly: "She is between 16 and 17 years of age, and is six months gone in pregnancy of her second child... She'll no doubt be the mother of a great many children ...; and that is a consideration to a purchaser who wants to raise a fine young stock." [143] It was usual pretty thoroughly throughout the South of that period for the slave advertisements to be shot through with such phrases as

[141] *Ibid.,* p. 74.
[142] *Ibid.,* p. 81, note 37.
[143] Ebenezer Davies, *American Scenes and Christian Slavery,* p. 56.

"child bearing women," "breeding slaves," "breeding period," "too old to breed," and the like.

Religion of the period—as religion of any period has ever very conveniently been able to do on any issue of important economic proportions—found itself quite capable of squinting at the practise of slave-breeding, a practise which would seem to be in direct opposition to some of its fundamental tenets; it seems to have had no ethical aspects at all. Even though the Reverend Jesse H. Turner, who gave up a Richmond pulpit to conduct very successfully a plantation, did not indulge in slave-rearing, it apparently did not occur to him to make a virtue of the fact by proclaiming it to issue from religious grounds, for he explained his prosperity merely by saying: "I keep no breeding woman or brood mare. If I want a negro I buy him already raised to my hand, and if I want a horse or a mule I buy him also... I think it cheaper to buy than to raise. At my house, therefore, there are no noisy groups of mischievous young negroes to feed, nor are there any flocks of young horses to maintain." [144] So little was religious sentiment opposed to the business of slave-breeding that it caused no comment for a church to reap direct benefit from it. "In 1767 some members of Presbyterian churches in Prince Edward county, Virginia, subscribed a sum of money and purchased two slave girls. These and their descendants were annually hired out and 'the hires appropriated to the payment of the salaries of the [common] pastor,'

[144] Ulrich B. Phillips, *Life and Labor in the Old South,* pp. 173-174.

till 1835, when they numbered about seventy. Then the owners, believing that it would be better for the slaves, ordered their sale and the investment of the money obtained. It was a very lucrative religious enterprise." [145]

But the propagation of slaves was by no means always left to proceed spontaneously; various lures and baits were offered to promote their increase. "The wife of a Georgia planter wrote that 'many indirect inducements [are] held out to reckless propagation, which has a sort of premium offered to it in the consideration of less work and more food counterbalanced by none of the sacred responsibilities which hallow and ennoble the relation of parent and child; in short, as their lives are for the most those of mere animals, their increase is literally mere animal breeding, to which every encouragement is given, for it adds to the master's livestock and the value of his estate.'" [146] However, such a procedure was in no sense novel, but was used by the Romans many centuries before America was ever dreamed of. Columella, writing in the first century, states in his *De Re Rustica* (I, viii, 18) that the gains from birth are to be regarded as ample grounds for encouraging the unions of slaves, and he thought that mothers should be rewarded for fecundity by a lessening of labor or even by freedom.

But not infrequently mere inducements towards and rewards for increase of the slaves were not considered enough, and masters would employ various forms of

[145] F. Bancroft, *op. cit.*, p. 87.
[146] *Ibid.*, p. 75.

actual coercion to force their slaves to breed. Writing of Colonial North Carolina, John Brickell asserts: "It frequently happens, when these [slave] women have no Children by the first Husband, after being a year or two cohabiting together, the Planters oblige them to take a second, third, fourth, fifth, or more Husbands or Bedfellows; a fruitful Woman amongst them being very much valued by the Planters, and a numerous Issue esteemed the greatest Riches in this Country."[147] At a much later date, Olmsted was informed by a Southerner: "Planters command their girls and women (married or unmarried) to have children; and I have known a great many negro girls to be sold off, because they did not have children. A breeding woman is worth from one-sixth to one-third more than one that does not breed."[148] That methods of continually changing Negro matings in an attempt to strike fertile unions must have been fairly common, is borne out by a free Negro's comment to Phillips: "If I had lived in slavery times my master would have given me half a dozen wives and taken care of all the children."[149] But the most amusing instance of forced breeding, or rather the attempt of it, that I have been able to find is related by John Josslyn and occurred around 1636 in Colonial Massachusetts:

"Mr. Maverick's negro woman came to my chamber window and in her own country language and tune sang

147 John Brickell, *The Natural History of North Carolina*, Dublin, 1737, p. 275.
148 Olmsted, *A Journey in the Seaboard Slave States*, p. 55.
149 Ulrich B. Phillips, *Life and Labor in the Old South*, p. 203.

very loud and shrill. Going out to her, she used a great deal of respect toward me and willingly would have expressed her grief in English. But I apprehended it by her countenance and deportment, whereupon I repaired to my host to learn of him the cause, for that I understood before that she had been a queen in her own countrey, and observed a very humble and dutiful garb used toward her by another negro who was her maid. Mr. Maverick was desirous to have a breed of negroes, and therefore seeing that she would not yield to perswasions to company with a negro young man he had in his house, he commanded him, will'd she nill'd she to go to bed to her—which was no sooner done than she kicked him out again. This she took in high disdain beyond her slavery, and this was the cause of her grief." [150]

Slave-breeding on the old plantations, after it had become a recognized business, sometimes took on a definite routine under the more systematic planters. Dr. Ferguson, a descendant of a line of planters, told Bancroft in 1902: "My grandfather took special care of the pregnant women and early put them on lighter work. As soon as the infants were weaned they were sent off to Mississippi City to be cared for by some of the old women. When they were strong enough to be 'watertoters' they were brought back to the plantation to work. As a rule, the planters down there did not want breeders; but those that did would encourage their slaves to

[150] John Josslyn, *Account of Two Voyages to New England,* in the Massachusetts Historical Society *Collections,* XXIII, 231, cited by U. B. Phillips, *American Negro Slavery,* p. 361.

pair off, would fix them up with a house and tell them that they would be sold if they did not have a baby in a year. Sometimes my grandfather would buy several women at a time. He had them carefully examined by a young physician who was his special friend."[151]

The actual revenues derived from the business of slave-rearing varied somewhat according to locality and period, but in the later days of slavery the profits became considerable. "Between 1830-1860, according to the year and the region, each babe in arms added from $100 to $200 or more to the value of its slave mother. It was the reverse in Massachusetts in colonial days: slavery there being unprofitable, the infants were considered an encumbrance and, when weaned, were given away like puppies. In the 'fifties, average boys or girls from 8 to 12 years old would bring at least $400 to $500; the best sometimes more than twice that much."[152] The well-known multiplying powers of the Negroes stood the masters in good stead, serving to heap up dividends for them. "In the number of their children the Negro women rivaled the remarkable fecundity of their mistresses. One phenomenal slave mother bore forty-one children, mostly of course as twins; and the records of many others ran well above a dozen each."[153]

Such occurrences were the exception, of course, but a steady, reasonably large increase could usually be depended upon. "Conservative estimates placed at from

[151] F. Bancroft, *op. cit.*, p. 76, note 25.
[152] *Ibid.*, pp. 78-79.
[153] Ulrich B. Phillips, *Life and Labor in the Old South*, p. 204.

four to eight per cent the average net annual value of the natural increase of the slaves on a plantation, apart from the advance in price, which was fully as much more."[154] But these figures are indeed conservative. "Ruffin estimated that a gang of slaves on a farm would normally increase fourfold in thirty or forty years. Mrs. Catterall cites from court reports many cases of fecundity like these: Nancy bore 17 children in 18 or 19 years; in an indefinite time Hannah had borne 14 or 15; another 'negro woman had 13 children, three of whom were sold'; another died in 1853, leaving 10 children ...one sold, and 'Sue, giving birth to a child every two years.' An ante-bellum physician in Tuskegee, Alabama, mentioned a case to the author where 'a single negro couple brought a $25,000 increase in forty years'; and an old planter and former Confederate officer met there remarked: 'As soon as a man had the money he bought a girl, and before many years she had a family that was worth $10,000.' Howell Cobb's slaves multiplied 'like rabbits' and were expected to double in number every ten or twelve years."[155]

And so it went. The Biblical injunction to "Be fruitful!" was enforced to the utmost by the planters on their slaves, but scarcely in conformance with the reasons for which that admonition was given. The sexual slavery of the American Negro in the old South shows him preeminently as a victim of the white man's lust: his fleshly lust and his money lust.

[154] F. Bancroft, *op. cit.*, p. 79.
[155] *Ibid.*, pp. 86-87.

VI

WHITE SLAVERY

1. Definition and General Considerations of White Slavery [156]

T H E study of white slavery and the white slave traffic
has at all times been vexed, both in lay and scholarly
circles, by its common confusion with prostitution, the
two terms often being used interchangeably and considered, and treated, as very nearly synonymous. Naturally, white slavery is inescapably bound up with
prostitution—and this holds, to varying degrees, for the
whole of the history of prostitution, though not recognized under that name until recently,—but there is a
great portion of the field and business of prostitution
that has no least concern with white slavery, and as the
chief common feature between the two is the *immoral
traffic in female bodies for gain* and little else of agreement, there is small point or profit in treating the two

[156] Be it understood that throughout this chapter deals in the
main with white slavery at its period of greatest activity, say,
the first fifteen years of this century, with the high point around
1910. Though at times, in the interest of more fluent compo-
sition, I may seem to speak of present conditions, I do so actually
only when I specify it quite clearly.

intermingledly; hence, we shall as much as possible treat white slavery as a separate and distinct phenomenon. My authority for such a stand needs no other basis than the simple fact that whereas prostitution shows on the whole no very marked decline, white slavery is greatly on the wane and will, according to present indications, eventually pretty thoroughly die out. If the two were closely intimate and highly necessary to each other they would have to stand or fall together. Prostitution is, at bottom, a form of employment, a means of livelihood for the women practising it; white slavery, like any other system of bondage or compulsory servitude, is a form of exploitation in which the profits go not to the worker but to the exploiter. The fact that the commodity handled is in both cases the same means little and certainly does not make the trades identical, no more than the work of hired farm hands and that of Negro plantation slaves can be considered of the same kind merely because both are agricultural labor. Thus, it is fallacious to envisage prostitution as all one; rather is it composed of two major branches: primary, in which the woman herself chooses to be a prostitute; and secondary, in which the woman is tricked or forced into being a prostitute by any of a great variety of means or circumstances. It is to the second branch, of course, that white slavery belongs.

This duality in the traffic in sensuality has existed since remote antiquity. The free, independent courtesans (as the ancient hetæræ) led quite comfortable existences and received a fair amount of respect, or at least respectful tolerance; but the low, mean, poorly paid prostitutes were usually slaves or otherwise were categorized in the slave class.[157] As the centuries marched on, their political or civic status gradually grew, but their actual and economic conditions remained the same. Thus we find that in ancient Rome "the feminine factor [of vice] was made up chiefly of the vast number of slave women, captured in the increasing wars of conquest." During the Middle Ages "the feminine factor [of vice] was largely composed of women abducted by robber bands, captured in petty wars and abused by the soldiery, and of the neglected offspring of these unfortunates." Now, in modern times, "the feminine factor [of vice] consists of women and girls from the midst of the social organism who have been impelled by circumstances to make a quasi-voluntary choice of prostitution as a means of livelihood. Speaking generally, we may say that the ancient prostitute was a slave, the mediæval prostitute an alien, the modern prostitute is a citizen."[158] This statement is true of the evolution of her political condition, but she is always a slave, a victim of circumstances. And primarily a slave of any sort is nothing more than a victim of circumstances, the circumstances of war, conquest, birth, nationality, wage conditions, and the like; and a sexual slave may be so as a result of all these and many other circumstances.

[157] See chap. II for some account of slaves and prostitution in antiquity.
[158] *The Social Evil,* a report prepared by The Committee of Fifteen (of New York City), N. Y., 1902, pp. 5-6.

White slavery, while not being identical with prostitution, though undeniably connected with it, is also
an important part of sexual slavery, but again is not at
all identical with the broader phenomenon, as this volume should adequately demonstrate. In fact, the field of
white slavery might be very neatly outlined by describing
it as that portion of human activity included in both
the sphere of prostitution and that of sexual slavery.
Naturally, such activity is bound to be world-wide and
not restricted to any one locality or country, but as in
this volume we are concerned primarily with America,
our treatment of white slavery shall also be restricted to
its manifestations in that country.[159]

There are some curious aspects to the subject of white
slavery, quite apart from its intrinsic interest. For one
thing, despite the fact of its having been carried on
under various forms since ancient times, the public at
large seemed totally ignorant of its existence until quite
recently. Suddenly, in the early years of this century,
public consciousness of the widespread "traffic in girls
and women" burst forth like a bombshell. People so
devoted themselves to wallowing in the horror and shame
of the business that they had no time or inclination to
investigate carefully and judiciously its real and exact
features and scope. Like all suddenly discovered abuses,

[159] For a good, brief summary of the high-lights in the international white slave traffic, as well as for a short bibliography of
works giving further details of the subject, see Iwan Bloch, *The
Sexual Life of Our Time*, trans. by M. E. Paul, N. Y., 1928, pp.
336 ff.

the attention it received was noisy and hysterical, instead of calmly but carefully and persistently inquiring as it should be in order best to cope with it, and consequently there was much futile fanning of the air and pawing of the ground. From doggedly believing nothing at all of a situation, people readily swing to believing many times the actual facts. Quite as might be expected, the hysterical awakening to the existence of white slavery gave rise to many foolish actions and movements and ridiculous overstatements of fact, just as the natural reaction to this later found men to deny everything completely, including the very existence of white slavery. It is now our difficult task to tread the devious paths of data, so tortured and obfuscated by the effusions and explosions of rabid and all too vocal reformers, and attempt to discover the true lineaments of actual fact. For the horror and shame of the matter is no part of our present concern with it; ours is a scholar's interest, a desire to arrive at as nearly a true picture of conditions as they were and are as is possible. And if failure be the result, let at least a portion of the blame descend on the shoulders of those well-meaning but misguided gentlemen of two decades past whose prolixity kicked up so thick a literary dust that it has as yet not completely settled.

One of the best evidences of the hysteria attending the early discussions of white slavery is the fact that scarcely any two writers or reformers of the period agree on just what was included under the term "white slavery." For example, we find such narrow and totally meaningless definitions as the following: "By the white slave trade is meant commerce in white women and girls for wicked purposes. Most of its history cannot be written, for two reasons: That these crimes are kept secret as far as possible, and that they are so revolting that their details cannot be published and ought not to be read anywhere outside of the bottomless pit."[160] Following this preamble are very nearly five hundred pages devoted to detailing and exposing the crimes of white slavery! An equally narrow and even more curious explanation of the term is proffered by a former Police Commissioner of New York City: "The white slave, as we use the term in the police business, is a woman whose earnings are collected by a man."[161] This would make white slaves of most wives who work to support unemployed husbands, as well as not a few daughters who are earning livings for indolent fathers. Again, we find it stated that by "white slavery" is understood "a system of procuring women and girls for prostitution by means of fraud or violence, and of transporting and detaining them in vice resorts against their will. Sometimes the term has been loosely applied to cover all phases in the traffic of women and made to include cases where the girls remain in the business not unwillingly, although unquestionably many of them are exploited and abused by those who derive profit from them. The latter meaning would extend the term white slavery to include practically the whole field

[160] Ernest A. Bell, *Fighting the Traffic in Young Girls,* 1911, p. 19.
[161] Gen. Theo. A. Bingham, *The Girl That Disappears,* Boston, 1911, p. 17.

of commercialized vice. In this sense the meaning is much broader than that in which it is used in international agreements regulating the trade in women."[162] The tendency to employ the term in increasing degrees of looseness is in great part responsible for the common confusion between white slavery and prostitution, which was mentioned earlier.

But we still have not touched upon all aspects of the traffic; other definitions we may find in plenty, and each of the subsequent ones gives us additional features to round out the picture, as in this: "The white slave traffic is the widely accepted term for the procuring, selling or buying of women with the intention of holding or forcing them into a life of prostitution. The term is not fairly descriptive, since the traffic reaches to every race and color, originating in Europe, where its victims are white, but it is generally used to designate the system by which vice markets are kept supplied."[163] This is the statement of a chairman of the National Vigilance Committee for the Suppression of the White Slave Traffic, and should be authoritative. It presents an important point in that the traffic does not necessarily concern only white women. It is substantiated in this by the Vice Commission of Chicago: "The term 'white slave' is a misnomer. As a matter of fact the traffic is not confined to white girls, but to all unfortunate girls and

[162] Howard B. Woolston, *Prostitution in the United States*, vol. I, N. Y., 1921, pp. 159-160.
[163] O. Edward Janney, *The White Slave Traffic in America*, N. Y., 1911, p. 13.

women of all colors, races and nationalities. The use of this term, however, is authorized by the National Government and was incorporated in the international law on the subject. A 'white slaver' in reality is a man who employs men or women or goes out himself to secure girls upon false pretense, or misrepresentation, or when the girl, intoxicated or drugged, and not in possession of her senses, is conveyed to any place for immoral purposes.

"If the girl is wayward and goes of her own free will she would not be a white slave in the true sense of the word; or the man or woman who induced her to go or accompanied her to an immoral place a 'white slaver.'"[164] The matter of the presence or absence of choice on the part of the girl or woman is, of course, all important, a point which is certainly made none too clear by Roe—who should assuredly be informed on such things—where he asserts that "white slavery is the procuring, either *with* or *without* their consent, of girls and women for immoral houses and for lives of shame and detaining them *against their wills* until they become so accustomed and hardened to lives of vice that they do not care to leave, become diseased, or too ashamed to face decent people again."[165]

After such an agglomeration of overstatements, understatements, and mis-statements, it is a distinct relief to

[164] *The Social Evil in Chicago*, by the Vice Commission of Chicago, Chicago, 1911, pp. 40-41.
[165] Clifford G. Roe, *Panders and Their White Slaves*, N. Y., 1910, p. 94. (Italics not in original.)

encounter an adequate and yet concise description of the white slave traffic: "As used in treaties between different countries and in federal and state legislation, the term implies procuring and transferring girls and women for prostitution. Whether or not they have been previously chaste, whether drawn by promises or forced to submit to prostitution, whether procured by one individual or a group of men working with a community of interest, whether turned over to other procurers, sold or placed in resorts of vice, girls procured and exploited through prostitution are just as truly victims of this hideous trade." [166]

The origin of the term "white slavery" itself is in some dispute. Clifford G. Roe, former assistant State's Attorney for Illinois, one of the earliest and probably the chiefest of the figures in the fight against the white slave traffic, is commonly credited with having first adopted the term in this country for current use and having popularized it. [167] This is possible; and such an act was a great boon to the American public for it enabled them to speak of an otherwise "unmentionable" subject. But the attempt sometimes made to attribute the first introduction of the designation to Roe is groundless. It has recently been asserted [168] that early in this century Roe was brought a note, picked up by a policeman, that had been flung from the window of a "crib" by a girl being held there.

[166] Maude E. Miner, *Slavery of Prostitution*, N. Y., 1916, p. 88.
[167] *New York Times*, June 28, 1934, notice of Roe's death.
[168] *Sunday Mirror*, Sept. 23, 1934, p. 15, art. " 'White Slaves' under the New Morals," by E. J. Hopkins.

This note read: "Help me—I am held captive as a white slave." The episode of the note may quite possibly be true, but the writer of this article draws upon his imagination when he declares that: "This was the first time the term 'white slavery' had been used, and it flashed all over the nation, greatly inflaming people's imaginations." As a matter of fact, the term grew out of the early international negotiations and treaties over the traffic in women and derives from a French expression, "Traite des Blanches" [literally: *trade in white women*], used in Paris in 1902 at the conference of fifteen European nations in contrast to an earlier phrase, "Traite des Noires," which had been employed a century previously in a convention held for the suppressing of the African slave trade. The British Government translated the French term as *White Slave Traffic* or *Trade,* and in America it achieved the form of *White Slavery.*[169] Thus, the early, or even first, usage of the final form of the expression may possibly be attributable to Roe, but even so it is a far cry from having invented it.

On this matter of the American coinage of the term, a speaker before the Second Pan-American Scientific Congress, held on December 30, 1915, at Washington, D. C., Mr. James Bronson Reynolds, said: "It has been charged that the term was the fabrication of sensational newspaper writers or of sentimental philanthropists of America. The charge evidently is not founded on fact. On the contrary, the designation evidences that at least one of the high contracting parties of the European

[169] H. B. Woolston, *op. cit.,* p. 159.

congresses, Great Britain, considered that the trade was one involving virtual slavery, while the continental countries adhered to the designation Traite des Blanches, or trade in women, a term clearly implying that the women, as objects of barter, had no free part in the transaction." [170]

Though we are here occupied in the main with the American phase of white slavery, the question obtrudes itself as to whether the unfortunates caught in this traffic are chiefly American women or are foreign women tricked in their own countries by panders and imported to this side of the water. Again we find great diversity of opinion, due largely to confusion and misunderstanding of the issues. Thus, we can find the number of foreigners exploited minimized in such statements: "You've heard of 'importing women for immoral purposes.' You hear it from pulpit, press, rostrum and street corner. Dimly you understand that there is an organized traffic in the living bodies of women—women from across the seas. That's about one-quarter of the truth. Seventy-five per cent of inmates of American houses of prostitution are *American* girls... It costs less to 'break' an American girl than to import and break an alien. Therefore, most of the victims are native Americans, 'the children of very poor parents.' " [171] Here once more is evidenced the ever-present identification of prostitution and white slavery: all inmates of brothels are by no means white slaves.

[170] *Ibid.,* p. 159, note 1.
[171] H. G. Creel, *Prostitution for Profit, A Police Reporter's View of the White Slave Traffic,* St. Louis, Mo., 1911, p. 9.

On the other hand, there is the following, directly opposed estimate of the situation: "My observation and the police records convince me that fully ninety-five per cent. of all the so-called white slaves are foreigners, principally girls from France, Italy, Germany and Hungary. Very few of them understand English at all. This is necessarily so. It is part of the system to keep them ignorant of the language, ignorant of American customs, ignorant of their rights under American law. Otherwise, their masters would have difficulty in keeping them under subjection." [172]

This conclusion, too, exhibits the ear-marks of snap judgment. In the first horror of America's discovery of its white slave traffic it was quite to be expected that it react in its normal fashion and attribute the bulk of the abuse to "them furriners," thus leaving America's proverbial intrinsic purity unimpugned. "There have been great waves of moral indignation, fostered by sensational writers, over 'white slavery.' Stories were told about elaborate organizations which kidnapped girls in Europe and kept them, against their will, in American brothels. It is true that the international exchange of prostitutes existed in the nineteenth century and continues to exist in the twentieth. But intelligently conducted surveys, both in Great Britain and in the United States, have shown the number of girls brought in from foreign countries by force or the use of trickery to be very small indeed. Most of the imported prostitutes in America pursued the same profession abroad and have

[172] T. A. Bingham, *op. cit.*, p. 16.

come here to improve their economic position."[178] So the true situation probably is, that the great majority of white slaves exploited in America were procured and enslaved in this country, but also that the greater portion of them are foreign-born girls, often recent immigrants, whose almost unbelievable ignorance, both native and as concerns American life and conditions, makes them an infinitely more ready prey to the wiles of the white slaver than any American-born girl could be.

Finally, the question as to just what are the underlying causes of the existence of white slavery, what are the motives for its practise and the reasons for its continuance, takes on a double aspect: what makes girls and women susceptible to the efforts of the white slaver, and what prompts the white slaver to prosecute his odious calling and enables him to continue in it? The answers to these queries are the same as those for many other abuses: MONEY! but in different connections in the two cases.

There is a multitude of things, naturally, that may tend to lay a girl open to the machinations of the procurer (and they will be gone into a bit more fully subsequently), but none, I daresay, can compare in importance with the influence of inadequate wages and evil working conditions. "There can be little doubt that economic conditions is one of the chief causes of the white slave traffic. The persuasions of the procurer are made alluring when they offer high wages to a girl who is out of a job, or to one who labors long hours for a pittance.

[178] Leo Markun, *Mrs. Grundy*, N. Y., 1930, p. 604.

Were it possible for every girl who needs work to get it at a fair rate of wages, the business of the procurer would be materially lessened." [174]

But the matter of the motivation and tolerance of the procurer is not so simple a matter. Of course, "easy money" is the basic spring of the whole affair, but it is by no means merely a question of the procurer's profits. "A study of the conditions that surround the traffic reveals the fact that it is not simply a case of the selling and buying of a human being against her will, but that the situation is an exceedingly complex one...

"To conduct the white slave traffic with success means that money must go to the house owner or tenant, the real estate agent, the saloon, the dance hall, the procurer, the police, the physician, the lawyer, many merchants, the telephone and messenger service and the transportation companies.

"It is not the 'demand and supply' which makes the public tolerate the white slave traffic and kindred evils, but ignorance, indifference, business interests and political expediency." [175] Vice, like war, will finally be wiped out only when it can be so arranged as to be not profitable to all not immediately concerned in its practise.

2. *Extent and Details of Operation of the White Slave Trade*

The actual magnitude of the white slave traffic, both at present and in former years, has been the subject of

[174] O. E. Janney, *op. cit.,* p. 93.
[175] *Ibid.,* pp. 79-80.

some controversy. People who, busily occupied with the routine of their daily lives, have never come into contact with any instances of the business, or else through their innocence have remained blind to any that might have passed under their notice, are inclined to deny that this trade goes on to any great degree. In the words of Edwin W. Sims, a United States District Attorney of Chicago: "There are some things so far removed from the lives of normal, decent people as to be simply unbelievable by them. The 'white slave' trade of today is one of these incredible things. The calmest, simplest statements of its facts are almost beyond the comprehension or belief of men and women who are mercifully spared from contact with the dark and hideous secrets of 'the under world' of the big cities."[176] This widespread incredulity, and often almost determined disbelief, on the part of the great mass of people to existing evils and abuses, make for the security and continuance of the evils and cause difficulties for and resistance toward overcoming them. This was especially evident in the fight waged against white slavery. As one woman active in the struggle against the traffic puts it: "One of the most disheartening things in the work of protecting innocent girls and restoring to useful lives those who have been betrayed from the path of right living is the blind incredulity of a very large part of the public. There are hundreds of thousands of women in the homes of this country who know as little of what is going on in the

[176] E. Norine Law, *The Shame of a Great Nation*, Harrisburg, Pa., 1909, p. 107.

world, so far as the safety of their daughters is concerned, as so many children. They are almost marvelously ignorant of the terrible conditions all about them—and all about their children, too."[177]

All this rather inhibits arriving at any sort of sane and accurate conclusion in regard to the actual extent of white slavery in America. Being a department of the larger, more general business of prostitution, it is to be expected that its volume would in general vary for different times and localities in accordance with that of the mother industry. This alters the problem to determining what percentage of prostitutes are, or were inducted into the profession as, white slaves. Says Roe: "A conservative estimate, perhaps, would put the number of those procured and exploited for immoral houses and apartments at fifty per cent of the total number leading lives of vice, or in other words about one-half are recruited through the white slave markets."[178] This figure, of course, is based on consideration of the means by which girls were first forced to practise prostitution, and does not mean that half the total number of prostitutes are being at present held to their trade against their will; after a certain length of time and degree of degradation a white slave, and particularly so in former years, has little choice or desire save to continue as she is.

Thus, it seems evident that an important feature in

[177] *Ibid.*, chap 9, "More About the Traffic in Shame," by Mrs. Ophelia Amigh, p. 132.
[178] Clifford G. Roe, *The Great War on White Slavery*, 1911, p. 171.

determining between a mere prostitute and a white slave is the nature of the cause of her first lapse into sexual irregularity. Once a girl has been "ruined" she may become an apparently voluntary prostitute, but if her "ruin" was first occasioned through force (for another's gain) or any form of exploitation she is essentially a white slave. Consequently, one must be wary of statistics on prostitutes that tend to show a negligible number of white slaves among them, for these figures are often compiled in such a manner (though usually unwittingly so) as to give the girl's reasons for following her profession under headings which superficially do not smack of white slavery at all, but many of which on examination reveal themselves as conditions of the girl's life or tendencies in her nature which make her ready game for the white slaver.

To illustrate this point, let us consider some actual tables of statistics on prostitution. We shall draw them from a very reputable and scholarly source: the Kneeland survey. This examination of prostitutes shows as the cause of the first sexual offense, the following: [179]

At first glance these tables may seem to imply that white slavery has a relatively small place in them, namely under "force," but when it is remembered that (as will be discussed later) a very common way for a procurer to win over and enslave a girl is by first gaining her love, and consequently her trust, it will be seen that the white

[179] This table is a composite drawn up from three tables in George J. Kneeland, *Commercialized Prostitution in New York*, N. Y., 1913, pp. 224, 238, 248.

slavery possibilities of the above listings advance greatly. Further, *weakness* and *physical predisposition* need not lead a girl directly into prostitution but may only render her susceptible to the enticements of the white slaver.

Cause	Cases in Bedford	Cases Outside Bedford	Cases from the Streets
Love	38.71%	37.86%	39.87%
Pay	20.43%	20.49%	24.33%
Force	22.22%	10.16%	5.51%
Weakness	8.24%	4.26%	3.07%
Physical predisposition.	.71%	6.72%	7.60%
Unknown	9.64%	20.49%	19.62%

The following table, cataloguing the reasons given by prostitutes for their having followed their line of business, perhaps demonstrates the point in question yet more adequately: [180]

(The figures represent the number of cases out of a total of 1011 cases.)

A. *In connection with her family*

   1. Neglect or abuse 41
   2. Immorality of parents 25
   3. Overstrictness 21
   4. Overindulgence 3
   5. Poverty 27
   6. Incompatibility (quarrels, nagging, etc.) 27

[180] *Ibid.*, p. 241.

7. Father, mother, or near relative put girl in life...... 6
8. Turned out of the house 18

B. *In connection with married life*
1. Incompatibility 8
2. Non-support 24
3. Immorality (including cruelty or criminality) 29
4. Desertion 12
5. Death 16
6. Husband put girl in the life 26

C. *Personal reasons*
1. "Ruined anyway" 15
2. Lover put girl in the life 80
3. Desertion by lover 33
4. White slave (put into life by force) 21
5. Bad company 108
6. Dances and shows 23
7. Love of excitement or a good time 58
8. Lazy, won't work 12
9. Love of money (a business enterprise) 3
10. Idle or lonely 0
11. No sex instruction 6
12. Ashamed to go home after first escapade 23
13. Not satisfied with one man 7
14. "Born bad"—enjoys the life 2
15. Previous use of drugs or drink 11
16. Stage environment 9
17. Tired of drudgery (usually housework) 16
18. "Easy money" 58
19. Love of clothes 7

D. *Economic reasons*
1. Can't support herself 67
2. Can't support herself and children or parents 37
3. Can't live according to her standards 17
4. Out of work, can't get work (often because of)....... 60
5. Ill health or defect 53
6. Not trained for skilled work and above unskilled.... 2

Now, by taking the above classification strictly at its face value it at once appears evident that the white slaves amongst this group of prostitutes form a negligible part of the whole, namely about 2 per cent. But if we examine the table with a broader, more discerning eye, we readily discover that such motives as non-support by the husband, desertion by a lover, bad company, no sex instruction, etc., may just as easily label the avenue of approach of the white slaver to the woman as it does her path to prostitution. With this in mind, it can be seen that fully half of the items above, or more, may serve to a greater or lesser degree as entering wedges for the procurer. Of course, such items as C. 13, 14, 18, etc., are distinctly out of the question and are the reasons only of the born prostitute, but looking at A. 5, 7; B. 2, 4, 6; C. 1, 2, 3, 5, 6, 11, 12, 16; D. 4, as well as some less obvious headings, we see that they may with equal facility apply to white slaves or prostitutes. The validity of this view of the matter will, I daresay, be much more apparent to the reader after he has perused the next section of this chapter, on the methods of procuring white slaves.

Thus, if instead of taking the figure shown by this table of 2 per cent of prostitutes as white slaves, we make a reasonable allowance from the other likely headings as probably contributing to this same category, we find that it will show remarkable agreement with Roe's estimate of 50 per cent of prostitutes being white slaves. So, in order to get at the number of white slaves in America, we have only to find the number of prostitutes there and take about half of that figure.

According to a 1934 Bulletin of the Division of Investigation, United States Department of Justice, there were held for prosecution during 1933 in a total of 762 American cities of all sizes, an average of 139 prostitutes per 100,000 of population.[181] Now, making some rapid, but to my mind allowable, assumptions, if we take it that only one out of every five prostitutes in American cities is held for prosecution in the course of a year, and if we make the moderate estimate that only two-thirds of the prostitutes in the country practise in towns and cities, and are therefore included in these figures, we readily arrive at the conclusion that the average city and country ratio is about 525 prostitutes per 100,000 population, or that one out of every two hundred persons in the United States is a prostitute, and consequently one out of every four hundred persons a white slave. The population of the United States being about 120,000,000, the number of white slaves in the country would then be in the neighborhood of 300,000. I am aware that many of the estimates employed in this calculation were made some two decades ago and that for various reasons white slavery conditions are not nearly as bad today as they were then; but this figure will still serve, I think, to give an approximate picture of conditions when white slavery was at its height (about 1910), the lesser population of the country being offset by the wider prevalence of commercialized vice. Present-day conditions of the traffic will be gone into in section 7 of this chapter.

Other opinions of the extent of the white slave traffic show the above figures not to be overly extravagant. It is held by one man—a man, it is true, rather inclined to

[181] *The World Almanac*, N. Y., 1935, p. 280.

see these things at their worst—that yearly there are 65,000 "daughters in American homes" and 15,000 foreign girls who fall prey to the traffic of white slavery.[182] If this be the annual addition to the ranks of pornial bondage, and it is taken into consideration that the average span of life of a girl caught in the traffic is estimated to be from five to seven years, it can be discerned that our own above calculations were not too far astray. Wilson's figure is supported by U. S. District Attorney Edwin W. Sims, who declares that from the evidence obtained in questioning some 250 girls taken in raids on houses in Chicago, he is led to believe that there were no less than 15,000 girls imported into this country as white slaves in one year.[183] More conservative estimates, naturally, are made by other authorities, but even a quite careful investigator places the number of girls procured each year in the United States at 25,000, and the number of men and women engaged in procuring them and living on their earnings at 50,000.[184]

Some conception of the extent of the traffic can be had by considering the number of deportations and exclusions from this country by the immigration authorities on the charge of connection with the traffic in women. It is known how inadequately such measures cope with the problem, so these figures, intrinsically small, never-

[182] Samuel Paynter Wilson, *Chicago by Gaslight,* Chicago, 1910, p. 35.
[183] E. A. Bell, *op. cit.,* chap. III, *"The White Slave Trade of Today,"* by Edwin W. Sims, p. 49.
[184] H. B. Woolston, *op. cit.,* p. 168.

theless represent a considerable volume of traffic in order
to enable them to attain even this magnitude. The following table [185] not only offers some representative figures
of this sort but also illustrates the greater strictness of
regulation in these matters by the government in recent
years as compared with former times:

	Procurers		Men living on earnings of prostitution		Women coming to U. S. for immoral purposes	
	Ex-cluded	De-ported	Ex-cluded	De-ported	Ex-cluded	De-ported
Prior to 1907	9	...	...	...	...	...
1907	1	0	...	...	18	...
1914	254	154	5	155	380	292
1915	192	101	7	58	219	204
1908-1915 inclus.	1435	...	...	...	2317	...

Summing this matter up, the Bureau of Immigration
reports that from 1892 to 1918 a total of 5,895 aliens
were debarred and deported for having connection with
the traffic in women.[186]

Likewise, an indication of the extent of the interstate
traffic in America may be obtained from the number of

[185] Table compiled from figures given by M. E. Miner, *Slavery
of Prostitution*, p. 116.
[186] H. B. Woolston, *op. cit.*, p. 162.

prosecutions under the White Slave Traffic Act, better known as the Mann Act. From the time of its enactment in June, 1910, to January, 1915, there were 1,057 persons convicted under it;[187] while from 1910 to July, 1916, there were 2,414 prosecutions instituted under it.[188] However, as is well known, not all of these prosecutions necessarily represent real cases of white slavery, but may in certain instances be merely a woman's attempt to blackmail some unfortunate man: that is the most lamentable feature of the Mann Act.

A matter certain to be of ripe interest to the average layman is the price at which the white slave is actually "sold" by her procurer or importer when he supplies her to the keeper of a house or "crib." The price brought by this commodity is subject to almost as many and as great variations as is the worth and attractiveness of the commodity itself, but is more directly affected by local conditions of supply and demand and in particular by the magnitude of expense incurred by the procurer in obtaining the girl. Agents of the Rockefeller Grand Jury, a special grand jury charged in 1910 with investigating white slavery in New York, arranged and actually effected the purchase of four girls from dealers in women: two of the girls cost $60.00 apiece and the other two $75.00 each.[189] According to the testimony of a white slave— she having been purchased for $50.00—the price at which girls were disposed of in Chicago varied from $25.00 to

[187] M. E. Miner, *op. cit.,* p. 118.
[188] H. B. Woolston, *op. cit.,* p. 162.
[189] T. A. Bingham, *op. cit.,* p. 29.

$100.00.[190] Yet another estimate strikes a broader range in both directions, placing the selling price of the girl anywhere from $15.00 to $500.00, being "generally based upon the beauty of the 'Slave.'"[191] Chinese girls seem for some reason to carry an especial value—which "value" has given rise to several quaint anatomical superstitions concerning them—and it is reported that these girls have been sold along the Pacific Coast at from $500.00 to $2,000.00 each,[192] while some of them are said to be worth from $2,000.00 to $3,000.00.[193]

As may readily be suspected, such variation in price is due in part to the existence of different kinds and degrees of "sale": the type of transaction that does little more than put a man in the way of a likely girl for his purposes, leaving the bulk of the actual procuring on his shoulders, will commonly be performed for a very modest sum; whereas the sort of deal that actually delivers a girl into a very real bondage will entail a quite large cash consideration,—and so proportionately between these extremes. The Immigration Commission summarizes the matter most aptly:

"It is, of course, impossible to state any regular price that is paid for girls, or the regular expenses of importing and placing them. The traffic is largely individual with both the importer and the girl, and the cost varies materially.

---

[190] C. G. Roe, *Panders and Their White Slaves*, p. 42.
[191] S. P. Wilson, *op. cit.*, p. 37.
[192] O. E. Janney, *op. cit.*, p. 32.
[193] H. B. Woolston, *op. cit.*, p. 168.

"The expressions 'buying girls,' 'selling girls,' etc., also vary in meaning. In order to test the assertions frequently made regarding the ease with which girls could be 'bought' at employment agencies for such purposes or could be secured through employment agencies for work as servants in disorderly houses, agents of the Commission applied to certain employment agencies, asking for girls to work in disorderly houses. Girls were delivered by employment agencies to a room hired for the purpose of making the test, for the payment of a $5 fee or even less; but in cases like this the employment agent is in no proper sense 'selling' the girl. He is simply paid a fee for his work as an agent, though he is doing a vile business.

"On the other hand, testimony shows that when an importer sells a girl to a disorderly-house keeper or to a pimp, and frequently into what is practically slavery, he often receives $500, and in certain cases twice or three times that sum, an amount sufficient to cover the expenses to which he has been put in securing the girl, his own expenses, and a substantial profit...

"Different still is the work of a man who as an agent lures a girl into a house where she is overpowered, or who, by false stories of profit and perhaps promise of marriage, seduces the girl and then delivers her in her misfortune into the hands of a keeper of a house of prostitution. Work of this kind is done sometimes for sums as low as $15." [194]

[194] Reports of the Immigration Commission, "Importation and Harboring of Women for Immoral Purposes," in *Senate Docu-*

The practise of white slavery as a business ordinarily falls into three major branches of activity: winning or procuring girls for the trade; getting or tricking them into houses where they can be subdued and exploited; and keeping the girls in the houses over a period of time despite their desire to leave.[195] As might easily be deduced from this arrangement, there are three chief types of person engaged in the traffic: the procurer, the person who, by fair means or foul, induces a girl to take up prostitution, or tricks or forces her to enter a house where she can be overcome; the importer or exporter, the person who undertakes to deliver to a house a girl who has already been procured, or takes her from one place to another, etc., as the exigencies of the trade demand— in short, a "dealer"; and the keeper of the brothel, the person who actually holds the girl to daily prostitution, keeping her in bondage and exploiting her to his own profit.[196] Of these, the procurer is undoubtedly the most active of the lot. It must not be forgotten, however, that the above arrangement is only typical and not invariable; in special forms of white slavery the pimp may work with or entirely replace the brothel keeper, and may even do his own procuring. But more of this anon.

Centers of activity of the white slave traffic seem to have been scattered pretty thoroughly through most of the large cities of this country, now one, now another

ments, vol. 19, pp. 53-124, Document No. 753, Washington, D. C., 1911, pp. 81-82.

[195] C. G. Roe, op. cit., p. 79.

[196] O. E. Janney, op. cit., p. 14.

rising into prominence. Three cities early important in the traffic were Chicago, Pittsburgh, and San Francisco. Chicago was a notorious den of iniquity around the turn of the century, and consequently a veritable gold mine for the white slaver. Turner, writing in 1907, says of it: "Chicago has it [the traffic] organized—from the supplying of young girls, to the drugging of the older and less salable women out of existence—with the nicety of modern industry. As in the stock-yards, not one shred of flesh is wasted." Conditions in Pittsburgh were so terrible that around 1903 Lincoln Steffens, the great corruption barer, investigated and exposed them. He found the whole traffic there closely controlled by ward syndicates that very successfully drained the miserable women of every cent they could lay hands on. He says most succinctly: "There are rich ex-police officials in Pittsburgh." [197] Corrupt politics and politicians have ever, to my mind, been infinitely more culpable in the matter of the white slave trade than the procurers and brothel keepers. But these three cities in no sense make up the sum of white slavery centers in America. "The chain," says former New York Police Commissioner Bingham, "has its largest center in New York and in Chicago, and branch connections in many other cities. It operates most freely in San Francisco, Los Angeles, Seattle, Nome, Alaska, Omaha, Denver and New Orleans." [198]

Of all American cities, however, New York appears to have achieved, at least in the early twentieth century,

[197] E. N. Law, *op. cit.,* pp. 49-56.
[198] T. A. Bingham, *op. cit.,* pp. 30-31.

special distinction as *the* headquarters of the white slave traffic in this country, being the point from which and in reference to which the majority of white slavers in other cities worked. Turner ranked it as one, perhaps the greatest, of the three principal centers of the white slave trade in the world, the other two being a group of cities in Austrian and Russian Poland, headed by Lemberg, and Paris.[199] It was estimated in 1908 by detectives of the Federal Government that half of the white slaves practising in America either originated in or entered the business through New York.[200]

To be sure, a factor that contributed in making New York such an element in this traffic is its being the chief port of entry to the country. Consequently, it is to be expected that the majority of white slaves imported from abroad would have had to have passed through this city. Truly, this foreign importation dwindled in later years as the immigration laws grew more strict, but at one time the getting of these girls into the country taxed the ingenuity of the white slavers. The Immigration Commission describes their methods of procedure as follows: "To secure entries into the country contrary to law, these immoral women or the deluded innocent victims of the procurers are usually brought in as wives or relatives of men accompanying them; as maids or relatives of women accompanying them; as women entering alone, booked to friends or relatives or to a home, and representing themselves as looking for work; as wives coming to men

[199] E. N. Law, *op. cit.*, pp. 72 & 78-81.
[200] *Ibid.*, p. 98.

supposed to be their husbands, or, in the case of Japanese, their proxy husbands. Many imported women are brought in by way of New York. Of late, many come through Canada. On the Pacific coast, San Francisco and Seattle are the chief ports of entry." [201]

Certain names, of course, stand out from the records as belonging to white slavers of extraordinary ingenuity, brutality, daring, or mere magnitude of operations. Such are Clarence Gentry, Andrew Lietke, Harry Frank, Louis Fleming, Gustave Lagerman, and others.[202] But three of the most prominent figures were: Henry Lair, who ran busy places in Chicago and San Francisco; Louis Paint, who was widely active in New York; and above all, Alphonse Dufour (or Dufaur) who achieved such infamous fame in Chicago.[203] This man and his wife, Eva, operated the largest white slave clearing house in that region, and probably in the entire country. It was not only a receiving and distributing station for the rest of the country, but was also a brothel where the girls were prostituted to the local trade. So great were the revenues from this establishment that when finally arrested in 1908 they were able to forfeit their bonds of $26,500 and escape to Paris. Their own books showed that their income for 1907 was $102,720, and for the first five months of 1908 was $41,000.[204]

The whole question of the white slave traffic has been

[201] Reports of the Immigration Commission, *loc. cit.*, pp. 68-69.
[202] C. G. Roe, *The Great War on White Slavery*, chaps. I & XI.
[203] T. A. Bingham, *op. cit.*, pp. 32-33.
[204] E. A. Bell, *op. cit.*, pp. 74-76.

needlessly confused by quibbles anent the "organization" of the agents throughout the country. In speaking of "organization" in this connection, the term seems generally to have been understood by those debating over it in the sense of a strictly formal, closely interconnected business system, much after the nature of one of our modern nation-wide mercantile corporations. Naturally, investigations for the purpose of discovering such organization—and there were such investigations specifically made, as that of the Rockefeller Grand Jury, of which more later—failed to find any. Though it was commonly found and freely admitted that the traffickers, while being essentially individual operators, were nevertheless held together to a greater or lesser degree by a community of interests, still city and police officials seem to have derived great comfort in the face of their inability or disinclination to cope with the problem by being able to pooh-pooh the whole matter with repeated assertions of the traffic's not being "formally organized." And yet they all were perfectly well aware that, for example, a New York procurer would be in touch constantly with men at different points throughout the country to whom he would send girls as occasion demanded; that procurers worked hand in glove in adjoining states; that one procurer would call on another if he had a sudden demand for girls that he could not meet; that in case a girl escaped from a procurer, others all over the country would, on being informed of it, be on the watch for her and help to return her to her "owner"; and that many other similar services of coöperation existed amongst them.[205] The making of such a futile issue is so obviously childish that I should hesitate to introduce it here had it not furnished subject matter for bitter debate for sedate, serious-minded gentlemen.

However, men closer to the facts than the theory of the traffic, those less interested in knocking over straw men they have set up, interpret the very obvious features of the situation somewhat differently. Such an one is former New York Police Commissioner, General Bingham, who in speaking of the white slavers says: "The men who own these women are of the lowest class and seem to have an organization or at least an understanding, which is national or even international in scope. We cannot get these men. If we could the whole white slave trade would drop and the whole social evil be intensely ameliorated, because these men work a regular trust."[206] Another writer goes even farther: "White Slavery has become a systematized business, gigantic in its scope, and powerful in its operations. It is claimed by judges of our courts that it has its 'Big Chief' and, that no less than $200,000 was made last year [1909] from the sale of young girls into a life of shame."[207] Again, former U. S. District Attorney for Chicago, E. W. Sims, speaks thusly: "It is only necessary to say that the legal evidence thus far collected establishes with complete moral certainty these

[205] M. E. Miner, *op. cit.,* p. 91; H. B. Woolston, *op. cit.,* pp. 160-161.
[206] E. A. Bell, *op. cit.,* p. 174.
[207] S. P. Wilson, *op. cit.,* p. 36.

awful facts: That the white slave traffic is a system operated by a syndicate which has its ramifications from the Atlantic seaboard to the Pacific Ocean, with 'clearing houses' or 'distributing centers' in nearly all of the larger cities." [208] All this testimony gives the quibbles about "formal organization" something of the appearance of an academic exercise.

The chief basis for the arguments against organization of the traffic was the findings of the Rockefeller Grand Jury, [209] but as they were especially charged to investigate that particular issue they could not very well avoid it. Their report was quite adequate, and though the circumstances forced them to report the absence of formal organization, they nevertheless so qualified this statement as accurately to give the real conditions; but the qualifications were lost sight of or deliberately ignored by interested parties, and the bald, general report of "no organization" was seized upon and made capital of. [210] In concluding this matter, allow me, by way of contrast authority to the Grand Jury's findings, to present a statement from a report of the Commission of Immigration of the State of New York:

"In the State of New York, as in other states and countries of the world, there are organized, ramified and well-equipped associations to secure girls for the purpose of prostitution. The recruiting of such girls in this country

[208] E. A. Bell, op. cit., pp. 56-57.

[209] See Appendix H for the Rockefeller Jury presentment.

[210] For further details of the presentation and misrepresentations of the Grand Jury's findings, see section 6 of this chapter.

is largely among those who are poor, ignorant or friendless. The attention of the Commission has been called to one organization incorporated under the laws of New York State as a mutual benefit society, with alleged purpose, 'To promote the sentiment of regard and friendship among the members and to render assistance in case of necessity.' This society is, in reality, an association of gamblers, procurers and keepers of disorderly houses, organized for the purpose of mutual protection in their business... The organization includes a membership of about one hundred residents of New York City, and has representatives and correspondents in various cities of the country, notably in Pittsburgh, Chicago and San Francisco." [211]

3. *Methods of Procuring White Slaves*

By far the most active person engaged in the business of white slavery is the procurer. It is through his indefatigable efforts that the constantly wasting ranks of white slaves are kept supplied with new recruits. Many women, of course, have followed this calling with success, combing and watching trains, boats, railway stations, docks, etc., for young and confused girls traveling alone who are likely to welcome a little "motherly" aid; but the boldest and most numerous operators are men. It is they who carry on their work in cheap dance-halls and other public places of amusement; it is they who lure girls from small towns under various pretexts, taking them from under the very nose of their family; it is often they who per-

[211] E. A. Bell, *op. cit.*, pp. 176-177.

sonally accomplish the "ruin" of the girl, degrading her
in her own mind so as to make her more pliant to their
purposes.[212] These and many other activities go to make
up the routine of the procurer's life. The Immigration
Commission found the business of procuring to be very
complex:

"This recruiting [of white slaves] is carried on both
here and abroad. The procurers, with cunning knowledge of human nature, play upon the weaknesses of vanity and pride, upon the laudable thrift and desire to
secure a better livelihood, upon the praiseworthy trust
and loyalty which innocent girls have for those to whom
they have given their affection, even upon their sentiments of religion, to get their victims into their toils; and
then in the pursuit of their purposes, with a cruelty at
times fiendish in its calculating coldness and brutality,
they exploit their attractions to the uttermost. If the
woman is young and affectionate, as often happens, the
procurer makes her acquaintance, treats her kindly, offers to assist her in securing a better livelihood. Her confidence won, she is within his power, and is calculatingly
led into a life of shame. If the procurer is a woman, the
innocent girl is usually promised pleasant work for large
pay."[213]

But to catalogue all the methods employed by the procurer would be an endless task; they seem to be limited
only by the exigencies of the occasion and the ingenuity
of the man. In a procurer's own words, as given in a con-

[212] M. E. Miner, *op. cit.*, p. 91; O. E. Janney, *op. cit.*, pp. 29-30.
[213] Reports of the Immigration Commission, *loc. cit.*, pp. 65-66.

fession: "We use any method to get them. Our business is to land them and we don't care how we do it. If they look easy we tell them of the fine clothes, the diamonds and all the money they can have. If they are hard to get we use knock-out drops." [214] However, despite the manifold variations in the technique of particular instances of procuring, there seem to be three general avenues of appeal by which the girl may be reached; they are: love, vanity, and ambition. Under the first heading comes all those cases in which the procurer first wins the love or affection of the girl, thus making her docile to whatever machinations follow. Vanity leads many girls to their undoing by allowing their desire for fine clothes, jewels, attention, flattery, etc., to blind them to the direction they are taking. Finally, ambition makes unsuspecting girls easy prey for the man who can promise them better positions, better pay, or opportunities for self-improvement of any sort. [215]

Girls, young and attractive, alone and adventuresome, are the procurer's object; he seeks them anywhere and everywhere. "Procurers frequent entrances to factories and department stores, or walk the streets at night striking up acquaintance with girls who are alone and looking for adventure. They select a girl waiting on a table in a restaurant, or at the cashier's desk, and gradually make her acquaintance. They attend steamboat excursions, are found at the seashore and amusement parks, in moving picture shows, at the public dance halls,—in fact, wher-

[214] E. A. Bell, *op. cit.*, p. 172.
[215] C. G. Roe, *Panders and Their White Slaves*, p. 79.

ever girls congregate for business or for pleasure. They choose with almost unerring judgment the type of girl who may be pliable to their will." [216] More definite data in this connection are embodied in the Immigration Commission's report on the traffic in women:

"A French girl seized in a raid of a disorderly house in Chicago stated to the United States authorities that she was approached when she was about 14 years of age; that her procurer promised her employment in America as a lady's maid or a companion, at wages far beyond any she could ever hope to get in France; that she came with him to the United States, and upon her arrival in Chicago was sold into a house of ill fame.

"The testimony of a girl of only 17 taken in a typical case in Seattle in 1909 shows some of the methods used in recruiting their victims by those engaged in the traffic. Flattery, promise of work, love-making, promise of marriage to a wealthy person, seduction without marriage, kind treatment for a month or two, travel with the procurer as wife, continual deception; then an explanation to the girl of the life awaiting her, which in her innocence she could not understand, experience in a house of ill fame in Montreal, Canada, personal brutality, even physical violence, being allowed not one cent of the hard-earned money; then transportation to Vancouver, to Prince Rupert, to Alaska, and to Seattle, in every city being forced to earn money in a shameful life, with total earnings of more than $2,000, none of which she was able to retain; finally release by arrest and readiness to be

[216] G. J. Kneeland, *op. cit.*, p. 86.

deported if only the story of her shame can be kept from her father and mother, sisters and brothers. This is but one of many such cases." [217]

So much for the general aspects of the *modus operandi* of procuring; let us turn now to a more systematic consideration of those types of procedure most effectively practised and commonly enough employed to define themselves from the vague "any way to get them" as typical procuring methods.

One thing always to be remembered about the white slave traffic is that it is fresh, innocent girls who are in the main sought after, partly because they are more easily taken in by the wiles of the agent, but chiefly because they are in greater demand. Consequently, the methods discussed here will deal with the trapping of innocent girls. As for the ready demand for such girls, it is well authenticated. "Many of the girls now engaged in prostitution have told agents of the Commission of the desire of procurers and disorderly-house keepers to obtain innocent young girls. They consider them particularly desirable because they have no pimp to demand a share of their earnings or to remove them from the disorderly house at will, and they will last longer, and therefore be more profitable. The proprietor of such a house will even pay a larger price for such a girl." [218] In this premium placed on innocent girls, coupled with the fact of the

[217] Reports of the Immigration Commission, *loc. cit.*, p. 67. For complete details of the case here referred to, see Appendix E, I, of the Report cited.

[218] *Ibid.*, p. 68.

supply of voluntary prostitutes being insufficient for the demand, can be found, I believe, much of the *raison d'être* of white slavery.

And in the procurer's search for negotiable feminine innocence, a most abundant source was found among young country girls. At the risk of charges of needless reiteration, let me pause again to remind the reader that I am writing of conditions of two to three decades past, when white slavery was flourishing and innocence had some existence to speak of outside the realms of melodrama and legend. Today, through the medium of better rural education, newspapers, radio, more readily accessible literature, and the like, the thoroughly innocent (or stupid) country girl is largely a memory. However, I have small doubt that at the period of which I write she populated the countryside in no small numbers; nor was her sheltered city sister much better equipped to cope with "sin" and "vice."

But to return to our subject, at one time the country girl formed a very important item of the white slaver's stock-in-trade. Those coming alone to the city to "make their way" were handled by much the same methods as were used on the city girls, the chief difference being that they would be likely to succumb more readily. Not content with this, however, procurers would travel the country, working one little town after another, picking up girls and laying foundations for later conquests. They might use any of a number of approaches, as may be seen briefly summed up by Roe: "When a pander strikes a rural community he must work very smoothly for generally every one knows that a stranger has arrived. He assumes the rôle of a drummer or a traveling man. Or perhaps he leads folks to believe he is a theatrical manager looking for new recruits. Then again he may pretend to be an employment agent bent upon securing help for some large store or factory. If he intends to work the 'love game' he is the son of a banker seeking rest and fresh air." [219]

Other devices for trapping the country girl there were in plenty, but one of the most popular was the frequenting of railway stations by the procurer and watching incoming trains for likely prospects, for poor girls, strangers in the city, coming there to seek work, and scraping acquaintance with them in some fashion and managing to have them accompany him on the offer of helping them to find their way about or obtain employment. The seasoned procurer could pick out likely girls of this type almost unfailingly, choosing the bewildered, frightened ones and leaving the independent, self-reliant ones alone. This type of procuring was especially suited to women operators, as the girls would turn more readily and completely to them and they could "mother" their victims into white slavery with a minimum of resistance. Another agent who in the early years preyed on girls of rustic origin was the cabman who, on being requested by the newly arrived girl to be taken to a suitable boarding house or hotel, would deliver her to a brothel where, once inside, she would be held and "broken in" to pros-

[219] C. G. Roe, *The Great War on White Slavery*, p. 154.

tution.[220] An operation of the same category as the above is the watching of the gangplanks of recently docked boats and the "spotting" and "cutting out" of promising looking immigrant girls who have journeyed to this country by themselves and who are being met by no friends or relatives.[221] In truth, the perils and pitfalls besetting the path of the innocent young girl trying to make her way in the big city, though hopelessly exaggerated and misrepresented in certain types of maudlinly lachrymose fiction of the early part of the century, yet had some very real existence and formed an ever-present danger necessary to be guarded against.[222]

But the country girls could by no means furnish material enough for the white slaver's activities; all classes of women received his attention and suffered from his depredations. Consequently, variety in the type of woman to be worked upon called for variety in the methods of procedure, and it was rare that the procurer was not able to meet the demands of the occasion.

Quite as would be expected, marriage offers a cover very commonly employed under which the traffic is carried on, and there are three main variations of its utilization. Possibly the most frequently used method of all

[220] *Chicago's Dark Places,* Chicago, 1891, pp. 127-129.

[221] E. A. Bell, *op. cit.,* p. 57.

[222] Typical fictionalized accounts of the difficulties and dangers that plagued the poor but pure working girl in the big city, may be found in such books as those by Virginia Brooks: *Little Lost Sister,* Chicago, 1914; *My Battles with Vice,* N. Y., 1915, etc.

is the promise of marriage. The procurer on winning the affection, or even love, of a girl will promise to marry her at the first convenient opportunity and on the strength of the reassurance of his promise will induce her to leave home and go live with him, after which her seduction and enslavement can be accomplished more leisurely in any of a number of manners. Marriage, even the promise of marriage, seems in some mysterious way always to make everything "all right"—much as when a man hesitates to relate a bawdy story in mixed company he is usually given *carte blanche* by those present when it is ascertained that all the women there are "married anyhow"—and consequently gives the procurer much freedom and great advantage in his subsequent persuasions with the girl. He may use his advantage to get her into a house where she will be forcibly detained and prostituted, or he may manage so to degrade and "ruin" her, especially in her own eyes, that she cares not or dares not to return to her family and former life.[223]

A second form of the marriage bait is false marriage. In this the procurer has some sort of ceremony performed over himself and the girl by a friend or a person who will hire out for such purposes, and the marriage license will be palmed off on the girl as the marriage certificate. After this, the method of handling the girl is not essentially different from that used under promise of marriage, save that the procurer will have much more power over the woman, she believing herself to be his wife and thus

[223] M. E. Miner, *op. cit.,* pp. 93-94.

bound to obey all his commands and wishes, even the most shameful.[224]

Finally, the procurer may even marry the girl legally in order to gain the power over her he desires.[225] It goes without saying that such a man has little compunction over the number of women he may marry; he merely says nothing of his other unions, changes his name as often as becomes necessary, and takes care that none of his "wives" talks too much. As most girls of the lower classes have been brought up to regard a husband as absolute lord and master of his wife in all respects, the man can often get her to do his will upon his mere bidding; or if he in any way forces, constrains, or mistreats her, the woman is not likely to make any complaint as she will believe the man to be entirely within his right as a husband.[226] A further advantage to such an arrangement lay in the fact that at one time according to the law of some states (as Illinois) a married woman could be held in an immoral resort, regardless of her youth, without its being possible to prosecute those holding her. Thus, often young girls, girls of fifteen, would be married off to some pander merely as a measure of safety for those exploiting her.[227]

The promise of material favors of divers kinds furnishes a fruitful field for the procurer's operations. The offer to help a girl to a position, or a better position, to

[224] *Ibid.*, pp. 94-96.
[225] O. E. Janney, *op. cit.*, pp. 24-25.
[226] M. E. Miner, *op. cit.*, pp. 96-97.
[227] C. G. Roe, *Panders and Their White Slaves*, p. 146.

higher wages, fine clothes, jewels, etc., has caused many an unsuspecting and over-ambitious girl to place herself in the hands of the person who dangles such tempting bait before her.[228] The appeal to a girl's vanity, ambition, or hidden desires is always a sure means of obtaining her eager and unquestioning compliance to the procurer's suggestions, so that it becomes relatively simple for him to lead her into circumstances and places where she may be taken advantage of. This same system may be worked indirectly through advertisements for workers of various kinds: servants, waitresses, companions, chorus girls, etc. Upon applying, or after being there a short time, the applicants are gradually apprised of the real nature of the work expected of them, work, it is always pointed out, at which they can earn many times the amount they could at that for which they were first hired.[229] The "good position" game has been employed endlessly by the white slaver. E. W. Sims, in speaking of the confessions of white slaves who have been released by police action, remarks: "Again, there is...a remarkable and impressive sameness in the stories related by these wretched girls. In the narratives of nearly all of them is a passage describing how some man of their acquaintance had offered to 'help' them to a good position in the city, to 'look after' them, and to 'take an interest' in them." [230]

At one time, the unscrupulously conducted employment agency was a veritable recruiting station for white

[228] M. E. Miner, *op. cit.*, pp. 100-102.

[229] *Ibid.*, pp. 97-98.

[230] E. A. Bell, *op. cit.*, p. 51.

slaves. Likely girls applying there, or answering their advertisements, could be sent unaccompanied to bawdy houses without having their suspicions aroused, where once inside they could be detained and coerced in the most expeditious manner. Stage-struck girls were plastic material to such of these institutions as maintained a theatrical service. A further advantage of this method of procuring lay in its so readily furnishing specious excuses for sending girls to distant cities without alarming either the girls or their friends or families, and the desirability of sending a white slave away from her home city is obvious.[231] These spurious employment agencies became a crying evil in many cities, resulting in some cases in laws to curb and abolish them.[232]

On the whole, the most attractive and profitable hunting-grounds for the white slaver is furnished by the cheap amusement places of a large city. It is to these places that poor girls come bent on getting what little pleasure they can afford, girls whose daily existence is most narrow and who are seeking desperately for some small emotional outlet, and in this mood and under the conditions of the amusement resorts they are easily led in any direction that promises to better or brighten their lot, even if only for a short time, only a few hours.[233]

And of all amusement places, undoubtedly the large,

[231] O. E. Janney, *op. cit.*, pp. 102-103; M. E. Miner, *op. cit.*, pp. 98-100; T. A. Bingham, *op. cit.*, pp. 55-56.

[232] See Appendix C for N. Y. Employment Agencies Act as it pertains to procuring.

[233] O. E. Janney, *op. cit.*, pp. 97-99.

cheap dance halls prevalent in former years—as the "Castle Gardens" of the East Side in New York—were the scene of the majority of this sort of procuring. The most obvious and satisfying amusement of the poor girl is dancing; the difficulties of English, which would hold an immigrant girl from the simplest sort of social intercourse, would prove no barrier to her dancing with the "nicest fellers"; a most moderate price—in the old days a five-cent fee sufficed for a whole evening's dancing—obtained a maximum of enjoyment; the fundamental requirements for a poor, uncultured girl's pleasure: noisy music, lights, crowds, and movement;—all these things were here open to her and waiting for her. What a climax to a week of grinding work to be able to revel in all this on Saturday evening! Only one thing was often lacking to complete the blissful picture: personal, male companionship. And that is where the procurer came in. His program of operations is obvious: to scrape an acquaintance with an unattached girl; to offer to dance with her or teach her to dance; to buy her a refreshment; to talk with her and make her laugh; to see her home; to take her dancing again or take her elsewhere; and finally so to gain her trust and affection as to render her quite amenable to any of the usual procuring tricks, from promise of marriage to tricking her into a house where she can be overcome. Naturally, in the same category as the dance hall must be placed the large summer excursion boat.[234]

[234] E. N. Law, *op. cit.,* pp. 92-94; C. G. Roe, *Panders and Their White Slaves,* pp. 94-97.

Another place that offered many opportunities to the pander around the beginning of this century—though its danger to the youth of the country was quite likely over-estimated—was the moving picture show. The objectionable feature was rarely the pictures shown, but rather the place's general accessibility to the procurer's activities. Says former Police Commissioner Bingham: "There is only one objection to the moving picture theater, and that is that it is conducted in darkness...The cheap theaters, the nickelodeon, the motion picture places are to young children from fourteen to sixteen what the dance hall is to the older girls and boys...To these theaters with their atmosphere of darkness and obscurity flock the procurer[s]. No one can tell with any degree of accuracy how great his harvest has been, but it is certain that the dark theaters have been and still continue to be a terrible menace to the morals of young girls." [235] Naturally, the chief purpose of the picture theater was as a meeting place, a place for the procurer to scrape acquaintance with promising young girls; the actual procuring was done elsewhere by the usual methods.

Equally important, it seems, as a recruiting grounds for the white slaver was that out-moded American institution, the "ice cream parlor." This was probably more dangerous than the moving picture theater, for here the proprietor himself could work at procuring, a thing patently most difficult in the case of the theater, and the innocuousness of the wares dispensed there

[235] T. A. Bingham, *op. cit.*, pp. 59-60.

would attract the most respectable girls. E. W. Sims declares that a girl was likely to find these resorts to be "a spider's web for entanglement," and holds this to be especially true of those places run by foreigners. He continues: "Scores of cases are on record where young girls have taken their first step toward 'white slavery' in places of this character. And it is hardly too much to say that a week does not pass in Chicago without the publication in some daily paper of the details of a police court case in which the ice cream parlor of this type is the scene of some girl's tragedy." Nor does the city alone harbor this class of establishment, for he further asserts: "I believe that there are good grounds for the suspicion that the ice cream parlor, kept by the foreigner in the large country town, is often a recruiting station, and a feeder for the 'white slave' traffic." [236] In all probability, if white slavery were still rampant today the corner drugstore would more than have replaced the ice cream parlor in the field of the procurer's operations; perhaps the pander would even have driven out the drugstore cowboy, which would have been a blessing.

No opportunity seems to have been overlooked by the procurer if it gave the least promise of rendering him some return for his efforts. He has even worked among school children, sometimes aided by a corps of half-grown boys, and in many cases when he has not succeeded outrightly in enticing them, he has predisposed them to

[236] E. N. Law, *op. cit.*, p. 162. See also S. P. Wilson, *op. cit.*, pp. 63-66, for an hysterical denunciation of the "ice cream joints" of Chicago as dens of evil.

their future downfall.[287] But what appears to me as the most despicable form of procuring, and one that had some currency around the turn of the century, was the visiting of charity wards in hospitals by woman procurers, picking out indigent and friendless girls there who had no prospects for the future upon their dismissal from the institution, and taking advantage of their desperate situation to offer them help and work upon their recovery. Thus, when discharged from the hospital, the girls would deliver themselves directly into bondage.[288]

The catalogue of procuring methods is, I imagine, well-nigh unending. When all else fails, force and violence may be resorted to. The girl may be drugged, dragged off of a dark street, trapped in a cab, tricked into a house on any of a number of pretexts, and there beaten, raped, starved into submission, or threatened until fear of her very life compels her to comply to her captors' demands. However, so successful on the whole are the more indirect procuring methods that the percentage of girls obtained by outright force is rather small.[289] But on occasion the white slaver can act with astounding audacity; his very boldness often insures his success. I quote two typical examples of his daring exploits:

"Three young girls of good family and irreproachable character, attracted by a fortune teller's sign displayed near the boardwalk of a seaside resort, went into the

[287] T. A. Bingham, *op. cit.*, pp. 57-58.
[288] *Chicago's Dark Places*, pp. 129-130.
[289] M. E. Miner, *op. cit.*, pp. 102-104.

house with no suspicion of evil or thought of danger, and soon after their entrance found themselves behind locked doors. In insolent terms, they were told they could not go out, and that as they had entered of their own accord, their reputation would be ruined by letting that fact become known. Two of the girls were timid, but the third, fortunately, was equal to the occasion. By her coolness and courage, she secured the escape of all three from the clutches of a procurer.

"In another instance, a man seized a young married woman of excellent social position at a railroad station in a city where she was a stranger, and attempted to drag her into a carriage, claiming that she was his insane wife." [240]

In conclusion, permit me to quote at length a procurer's own confession of the technique of winning and trapping girls. Though it offers nothing very different from what we have already discussed, yet, coming from a man who obviously should know about these things, it lends a note of authority to the whole matter by confirming what has been already said:

"They [procurers] all have about the same system; only they change it to suit the girl. In the summer time they go out to the amusement parks and summer gardens around here. They also work the country towns and near-by cities. In winter time they roam about the large stores, attend nickel shows and dance halls, and get the girls in these places. Different methods are used according to the girl they are trying to get. Sometimes they

[240] O. E. Janney, *op. cit.*, pp. 23-24.

invite the girls to the theatre or out for a drive, or something like that, and 'con' them along by telling them that they are the sons of wealthy men or that they are representing some theatrical management, or something, —any way to get them. If the girl is one of the 'love sick' kind, they pretend they are in love with her, and in most cases they promise to marry her. If the girl is looking for a job, they are always 'Johnny on the spot' with an offer of a good position. The fellows offer the girls employment to their liking, which of course is a trick, which they never intend to carry out. The whole idea is to get the girl's confidence and the fellow will say anything in order to do this. I know fellows who have gone across the Lake to some of the summer resorts and got girls to come back with them, the girls thinking that they were going to go upon the stage, and in one case I know of, they took the girl out to measure her for a theatrical dress and put a 'house dress' upon her and in that way got her street clothes away.

"After they have handed out a line of talk and once got them started, if the girls are hard to land, they use 'knock out' drops. Sometimes they tell the girls they are going to take them out to meet a 'lady friend,' and if the girls are flighty and wayward the boys argue with them, telling them of the big money they can make. After they get them to their flats (clearing houses) they get the woman who runs a house to come over, and she shows the girl her diamonds and fine dress, and tells how easily the girl can get some like them without any work, and the girl is induced to go with her. But of course they could only do that when the girl has a sort of leaning that way and wants to see what the inside of one of those houses looks like.

"When the fellows make the girls think they are in love with them, they take them out to dances, dinners and the theatres several times, until they get the girls' confidence and then they finally get them to their flats, and later sell them into the houses.

"Sometimes they really marry the girl too, because they say they cannot arrest a fellow for putting a married girl into a house. One, for example, is Jack Daily. He married a girl by the name of Hazel. He took her to Indiana some place and married her, because they thought she was too young to keep in the house and he got paid for marrying her. Harry Balding knows all about it. There are lots of other fellows who have married girls, but I can't remember what their names are now." [241]

4. *Methods of Holding and Exploiting White Slaves*

Possibly the most difficultly comprehensible feature of white slavery to the average person's mind is the fact of its being able to hold girls against their wills and subject them to degrading lives in the midst of civilized communities. Why, it will be asked, does the girl not merely leave or make her escape in some fashion, as it is almost impossible to hold a person indefinitely outside a veritable jail-house or by keeping her firmly bound? And, surely, the exigencies of her exploitation demand that

[241] C. G. Roe, *op. cit.*, pp. 56-58.

she be not too strictly confined. And this line of reasoning is perfectly correct: in, say, two-thirds of the cases it is physically quite possible for the girl to get away; that is, there are no insuperable physical barriers (as chains or bars) against her escape. But the girl is firmly held by more subtle means, and though it may be argued that the devices used have no legitimate power, that legally they cannot bind or in any way control the girl, still they are effective because the girl *believes* or is made to believe that they are.

The men exploiting these women often have amazing, inexplicable powers over them, so that they will not even attempt an escape regardless of how good their opportunities may be. This power is quite apart from that which may arise from the woman's love for the man. It need not even be based upon any sort of physical admiration for the man: one of the most active procurers in New York was short, heavy, and humpbacked. Such a man will frequently boast that when once a woman comes under his influence she will do anything for him.[242] (I shall spare the reader that worn simile of the snake and the bird.)

But this, shall we say, hypnotic control of the girl is only one factor, and a relatively small one, of her subjection, which is achieved through a great variety of means. Undoubtedly, no one is better fitted to define these means than the Immigration Commission:

"The control of the man over his girl is explained in part by her real affection for him (in many cases he is

[242] G. J. Kneeland, *op. cit.*, p. 86.

her first lover), by the care which he gives her, by the threats which he makes against her, by even his brutality, and often beyond that there are many things that serve to make her condition helpless and hopeless. An innocent girl often revolts bitterly against the life and refuses to submit until compulsion is used. Then for a considerable length of time the man finds it necessary to watch her carefully until at length she is 'broken in'—the technical expression. After that, if she tries to escape, he may apply for aid to almost any other pimp in any city of the United States. These men are constantly traveling; they frequent the same clubs and are in close correspondence. If she has been seen by other men they make a business of remembering her, and her photograph, in case of escape, would be sent to other places. Not only do they wish to help one another, but they wish also to impress upon their own women the difficulties and dangers of attempting to escape." [243]

And when, as is frequently the case, the woman being dealt with is a foreigner, the white slaver's problem in controlling her becomes greatly simplified. In the words, again, of the Commission: "The alien woman is ignorant of the language of the country, knows nothing beyond a few blocks of the city where she lives, has usually no money, and no knowledge of the rescue homes and institutions which might help her. If she has been here long enough and has learned, through suffering, to become resourceful, possibly how to keep secretly a little money

[243] Reports of the Immigration Commission, *loc. cit.*, p. 76. See also, O. E. Janney, *op. cit.*, pp. 35-36.

for herself, she has often become so nervously weakened, so morally degraded, that she cannot look beyond to any better life, and apparently even loses desire for any change."[244]

The strangest of all the bonds by which the pander manages to hold women subservient to him is that of their love for him. Naturally, the man in winning an innocent girl over to his purposes often pays court to her and succeeds in arousing a very sincere love in her, a love that causes her to trust him and, through ignorance of the true state of affairs, to accede to his requests. But the amazing part is that many of these women, even after the man has been revealed in his true colors, after they have suffered from and seen his brutality and greed, after they have been beaten, degraded, robbed of all their earnings, and abused in all possible manners, still do very frequently retain affection enough for him to stay with him and serve his ends, despite many opportunities of escaping or bettering themselves. Truly, not a few of the women do eventually see the light and, having their love undergo a complete revulsion, either leave the man or institute his prosecution. But many of them, even when brought into court to testify against the man, say not a word, though their testimony would usually free them from their bondage. Such attachment on the part of the woman is most difficult to comprehend. "Her devotion to her 'lover' may be explained partly by her maternal instinct to lavish care upon some one, and partly by her sense of gratification with the presence of a person

[244] Reports of the Immigration Commission, *loc. cit.*, p. 76.

to whom she feels superior. Cast off by friends and degraded in her own estimation, she is still far above the wretched associate who lives upon her earnings. Then, too, though far from the ideal she had pictured, and much distorted, the relationship enables her to have something that stands for a 'home.'" Panders have been known to have six or more women all working for them simultaneously, all aware of the existence of the others, and apparently held to the man chiefly by some intangible sort of attraction.[245]

A far more tangible hold over a woman is a pander's promise of protection for her. He promises to shield her and prevent her being arrested or imprisoned. If she is arrested, he attends to getting her a lawyer or bondsman, paying her fine, or doing whatever can be done to free her. Naturally, a prostitute in prison is no profit to a pander, so it is to his best advantage to work her release, but the girl rarely realizes this and is duly grateful and faithful to the man in consequence.[246]

But the most obvious, and likely the most effective, method to be employed by panders to hold white slaves in their power is by the use of fear and threats. They are promised all sorts of dire and fantastic penalties if they try to escape or give evidence against their masters: they will be beaten, have their faces cut, be deported, be sent to prison, be thrown in the river or shot, or have any of a number of terrible things happen to them. Prostitutes have been brutally killed by panders and their gangs for

[245] M. E. Miner, *op. cit.*, pp. 113-116.
[246] *Ibid.*, pp. 112-113.

informing against them, or even for trying to leave the life they were leading, and these are always dangled before the eyes of the girls as "examples" of what will happen to them if they become contumacious, thus usually serving to terrify and subdue them.[247] A more subtle form of intimidation is at times utilized by threatening to write the girl's family if she shows any insubordination and apprise them of her condition. Many of the unfortunate girls would agree to any fate in the world rather than allow their people to learn of their degradation.[248]

An almost indispensable instrument of the white slave traffic is the house of prostitution. Prostitution can, indeed, be practised sporadically without it, by scattered prostitutes working for their pimps throughout the city, or working independently, but such a condition does not lend itself to a traffic in women. Once a house is set up a definite trade may be established: a more or less steady patronage is assured, thus justifying some investment, the proprietor can give procurers specific orders for girls, and the nature of the house and its fixed location lend themselves to the "breaking" of recalcitrant girls,—rather a difficult thing for a mere pimp who leads something of a nomadic existence. Consequently, the brothel keepers and the procurers are the typical white slavers (though many of the keepers do some of their own procuring), each dependent upon the other—the keeper for his supply and the procurer for his market—and both dependent

[247] *Ibid.*, pp. 108-112.
[248] O. E. Janney, *op. cit.*, p. 37.

upon the existence of the house of prostitution.[249] While the pimp can practise white slavery to an extent, it must be of a more indirect sort in which he maintains his control over the woman by some of the more subtle means listed above.

The brothel proprietor seems so much to have run to a type that an investigator has been able to furnish us with an average description of him: "If a composite photograph could be made of typical owners of vice resorts, it would show a large, well-fed man about forty years of age and five feet, eight inches in height. His clothes are the latest cut, loud in design, and carefully pressed. A heavy watch chain adorns his waistcoat, a large diamond sparkles in a flashy necktie, and his fat, chubby fingers are encircled with gold and diamond rings."[250]

It is only by means of the house of prostitution that the "breaking-in" system of subduing a recently recruited white slave can be employed in any sort of thoroughgoing and effective manner. To be sure, the procurer will make use of a certain amount of compulsion to gain control over the girl's mind and will, utilizing fear, threats, and brutal treatment in order to instruct her in the proper story she is to tell if questioned by the police and to deny all association with him, and to compel her to remain faithful and turn over all her earnings to him. But if the girl proves to be made of sterner stuff than the

[249] G. J. Kneeland, op. cit., pp. 85, 99.
[250] Ibid., p. 80.

average and shows herself unresponsive to such coercion that he as an individual can bring to bear on her, his only remaining course is to place her in a house where she can be systematically and thoroughly "broken in." [251]

The process followed in the houses seems to have pursued a fairly well established and uniform routine, at the end of which the girl was almost invariably quite meek and subdued, entirely pliant to the will of her masters. The general outlines of the process were as follows:

"Once enticed into a house, they are subjected to what is known as the 'breaking-in' process, during which they are at first kept as actual prisoners. They are not permitted to go out unaccompanied. They are then told that there is no other life open to them after such an experience, and that their relatives will not take them back (which is too true, in many cases). Their street clothes are taken from them, and they are supplied instead with short dresses or flimsy finery in which they cannot appear in the street. These garments and the jewelry with which they are provided are charged to them at exorbitant rates, and they are told—and believe—that they cannot leave the house until these things are paid for. When, however, the money is raised to pay for the clothes and jewels, the victim finds that by some means another and heavier debt has been charged to her. She is told that any attempt on her part to evade these debts will subject her to 'handling' by the police, followed by imprisonment and publicity. Intimidated by threats and ill treatment, con-

[251] M. E. Miner, *op. cit.*, pp. 105-108.

scious of her degradation, she in time accepts the conditions and continues a life of vice." [252]

Even after she has been "broken" and is being exploited with profit, the house continues to hold her in strict bondage by its system. By a combination of strict surveillance, intimidation, and constantly keeping the girl heavily indebted to the house, her escape, or even attempt to escape, is made highly improbable. Harry G. Parkin, an assistant United States district attorney in Chicago, has to report this example of successfully holding a girl in a house:

"In one of the recent raids a big Irish girl was taken and held as a witness. She was old enough, strong enough, and wise enough, it seemed to me, to have overcome almost every kind of opposition, even physical violence. She could have put up a fight which few men, no matter how brutal, would care to meet. I asked her why she did not get out of the house, which was one of the worst in Chicago. Her answer was:

"'Get out! I can't. They make us buy the cheapest rags, and they are charged against us at fabulous prices; they make us change outfits at intervals of two or three weeks, until we are so deeply in debt that there is no hope of ever getting out from under. Then, to make such matters worse, we seldom get an accounting oftener than once in six months, and sometimes ten months or a year will pass between settlements, and when we do get an accounting it is always to find ourselves deeper in debt

[252] O. E. Janney, *op. cit.,* pp. 36-37.

than before. We've simply got to stick, and that's all there is to it.' "[253]

There is a special variety of house in which white slavery is carried on and, while not as numerous as the more ordinary houses of prostitution, they offer an example of forced prostitution in which the "slavery" aspect is very real indeed. They are technically known as "cribs," and are adequately described by Janney:

"In many cities on the Pacific Coast there exists a form of woman slavery which, it would seem, needs only to be described to give rise to a movement for its destruction. There are erected large and flimsily built houses called 'cribs,' consisting of many small rooms opening into inner passages by means of a barred window and door, which is kept locked by the manager, the key being given to men as they apply to him. Within these little cells, scantily furnished, are kept young girls, most of them Chinese and Japanese, but some of them European and American. They have little light or air, are rarely allowed to leave their rooms, and the manager receives the money."[254]

In 1908 an extensive crib system was found to be in operation in San Francisco, there being houses in which as many as one hundred and sixty girls were held, while not a few other cities in California—as Oakland, Sacramento, Bakersfield, Stockton, San Diego, Watsonville, etc.—carried on the same business to a lesser degree. A

[253] Reports of the Immigration Commission, loc. cit., p. 79.
[254] O. E. Janney, op. cit., p. 41.

crusade of the citizens of Los Angeles did away with the cribs there in 1904.[255]

It may be well to pause here a moment to guard against a possible misapprehension and point out that though the house of prostitution is closely linked with white slavery, not all the inmates are of necessity white slaves nor have they all been placed there by means of procurers. Quite a few of them are voluntary prostitutes, women who have freely chosen or drifted into the life because they liked it or because to them it seemed the best of various dubious paths opening before them. But the supply of girls voluntarily entering immoral houses never equals the demand; hence, the difference is made up by white slaves supplied by procurers. The fact that the average span of life of a girl under the conditions in these houses is exceedingly short serves to aid in keeping the market in white slaves brisk and the procurer busy. Even if a girl does not die off as young as is generally the case, she rarely remains attractive enough for a house past the age of twenty-five, and so is dismissed to other, and baser, activities, thus leaving room for new material.[256]

Though white slavery, in the strict meaning of the term, is largely dependent upon a house of prostitution for its effective practise, there is, nevertheless, another form of immoral bondage carried on without the aid of a house in which the woman is constrained to follow her

[255] *Ibid.*, pp. 43-44.
[256] C. G. Roe, *Panders and Their White Slaves*, p. 108; O. E. Janney, *op. cit.*, p. 105.

trade not by material bonds and ties, but is firmly held and compelled by invisible fetters. This is the controlled street-walker who solicits her own clients, takes them to her own room, collects her own money, and attends to all the details of the transaction personally, but who in a variety of fashions is held subservient to a pimp who keeps her at her work and to whom she dutifully returns regularly and delivers her earnings.[257] This is a virtual bondage which makes her exploitation undeniably a form of white slavery. The means by which she is held in subjection are well outlined by Kneeland:

"In her relation to the pimp, as well as to the house madame, the prostitute is not infrequently to all intents and purposes a white slave. For the pimp, like the madame, subjects her in many cases completely to his will and command. This does not mean that the girl is necessarily imprisoned behind locked doors and barred windows. But restraint may be thoroughly effective, even though not actually or mainly physical. Uneducated, with little or no comprehension of her legal rights or of the powers which could be invoked to aid her, often an immigrant or at least a stranger, she is soon cowed by the brute to whom she has mistakenly attached herself. Should she make an effort to break away, she is pursued and hemmed in by the concerted efforts of her cadet and his associates. As a rule, however, pimps are skillful enough to play for and to obtain the sentimental loyalty of their women; so that the prostitute herself becomes

[257] O. E. Janney, *op. cit.,* p. 28.

the greatest obstacle to her own freedom and rehabilitation."[258]

An average description of the pimp might be somewhat as follows: somewhere between twenty to sixty years of age; tall, perhaps five feet, nine inches, or better; thin, decidedly underweight, often tubercular in appearance; brunette; dark eyes—brown or hazel; dark, sallow, dry skin; well cared for teeth; and, in two-thirds of the cases, American-born.[259]

It would scarcely be proper to close this section without briefly taking up a most distinctive type, quite common some years ago, who combined the offices of both the pimp and the procurer. I refer to that personage known as the "cadet," whose native heath, it seems, was New York, so we shall permit a committee from that city to describe him:

"The 'cadet' is a young man, averaging from eighteen to twenty-five years of age, who, after having served a short apprenticeship as a 'light-house,' secures a staff of girls and lives upon their earnings... His occupation is professional seduction. By occasional visits he succeeds in securing the friendship of some attractive shop-girl. By apparently kind and generous treatment, and by giving the young girl glimpses of a standard of living which she had never dared hope to attain, this friendship rapidly ripens into infatuation. The Raines Law hotel or the 'furnished-room house,' with its café on the ground

---

[258] G. J. Kneeland, *op. cit.*, pp. 89-90.
[259] B. L. Reitman, *The Second Oldest Profession*, N. Y., 1931, pp. 165-167.

floor, is soon visited for refreshments. After a drugged drink, the girl wakens and finds herself at the mercy of her supposed friend. Through fear and promises of marriage she casts her fortunes with her companion, and goes to live with him. The companion disappears; and the shop-girl finds herself an inmate of a house of prostitution. She is forced to receive visitors of the house. For each visitor the girl receives a brass or pasteboard check from the cashier of the house entitling her to twenty-five cents. The 'cadet' returns to the house at frequent intervals, takes the checks from his victim, and cashes them at the cashier's desk.[260]

The magnitude of the cadet's operations becomes apparent when it is discovered that some authorities believed that at least two-thirds of the prostitutes of the country were controlled by individual cadets, while they held the proportion to be much higher in New York City.[261] This figure may be a trifle high, but it graphically demonstrates that the cadet was no negligible quantity. Though a product of New York's East Side, the breed soon spread to other American cities, starting about 1901, the year of Tammany's defeat and the subsequent anti-vice tendencies. New York cadets were found in hundreds in San Francisco, and they were strong in Los Angeles until the time of the clean-up in that city, about 1908. In 1910, it was held that they swarmed in all the larger American cities, from the Alaskan frontier to Panama,

[260] *The Social Evil*, report by The Committee of Fifteen, pp. 183-184.
[261] E. N. Law, *op. cit.*, pp. 48-49.

from Boston to the mining regions of the West.[262] Naturally, the conditions that have acted to reduce white slavery in recent years have dealt similarly with the cadet.

5. *The White Slave's Existence*

Now, after having reviewed the scope and general features of the traffic in women and having studied the unit processes in the practise of white slavery, it would be desirable, I believe, to make a brief investigation of just what constituted the life and daily routine of a white slave and to attempt to discover if conditions were as terrible and inhuman under the system as has often been implied, or whether the situation was shocking principally to the æsthetic sense by reason of one person's exploiting the body of another, while the other person's existence was actually not too intolerable.

Popular writers on this subject—newspaper and periodical writers—have on the whole exhibited their usual failing in dealing with matters of wide-spread abuse: they either grossly exaggerate and magnify the whole situation, or they minimize it into insignificance; rarely, indeed, do they ever give a careful, uncolored report of conditions. In a recent series of three feature articles on white slavery appearing in a New York paper,[263] the writer rather pooh-poohs the old idea of white slavery as a condition of real bondage, asserting that the girls, while often not desiring the life, take to it as the best and

[262] *Ibid.*, pp. 87-88.
[263] *"White Slaves" Under the New Morals*, by Ernest Jerome Hopkins, *Sunday Mirror*, Sept. 16, 23, 30, 1934.

easiest way of earning a living and are held to it only by economic necessity. To be sure, this has always been more or less present as a factor, but there seems to be ample evidence that a very real sort of "slavery" existed for the unfortunate women caught in the system. This writer has probably made the error of judging conditions as they were in former years in the light of those obtaining at present. In contrast to this, we have former Police Commissioner Bingham's verdict that there is "absolutely no question of the existence to an appalling extent of women who are veritable white slaves." He further says that there are at least 2,000 of them brought into the country every year like cattle and disposed of like cattle.[264]

For a fair picture, in general terms, of the average treatment received by a white slave in a house, we may turn to the Immigration Commission:

"When placed in a house she is, in some cases, kindly treated by her man and the madam under whom she works, provided she is submissive and attractive and profitable. Her earnings may be large—ten times as much in this country as in eastern Europe. She may at times earn in one day from two to four times as much as her washerwoman can earn in a week, but of these earnings she generally gets practically nothing. If she is docile and beautiful and makes herself a favorite with the madam, she may occasionally be allowed to ride in the parks handsomely dressed; she may wear jewelry to attract a customer; but of her earnings the madam will take one-

[264] T. A. Bingham, *op. cit.*, p. 15.

half. She must pay twice as much for her board as she would pay elsewhere; she pays three or four times the regular price for clothes that are furnished her; and when these tolls have been taken little or nothing is left. She is usually kept heavily in debt in order that she may not escape; and besides that, her exploiters keep the books and often cheat her out of her rightful dues, even under the system of extortion which she recognizes.

"Frequently she is not allowed to leave the house except in company with those who will watch her; she is deprived of all street clothing; she is forced to receive any visitor who chooses her to gratify his desires, however vile or unnatural; she often contracts loathsome and dangerous diseases and lives hopelessly on, looking forward to an early death." [265]

It seems to me that under such circumstances the girl is being held by a great deal more than "economic necessity."

Among the older authorities on white slavery, those writing at the time the traffic was in full swing, we find not one dissenting voice to the general consensus that "white slavery" was no misnomer. Janney, the chairman of the National Vigilance Committee, states that to all intents and purposes the human chattels trafficked in were *slaves*, forced into prostitution, confined, kept under close watch, forced to do their master's bidding, and obliged to give him the money they received. [266] E. W. Sims declares that when once a girl is sold into a house

[265] Reports of the Immigration Commission, *loc. cit.,* p. 75.
[266] O. E. Janney, *op. cit.,* p. 15.

she becomes in every sense a prisoner; that in each of these houses is a room with but one door, the key to which is held by the keeper, in which is locked all the street clothes and ordinary apparel of the women.[267] The state of affairs in Chicago was fairly representative of those formerly to be found elsewhere throughout the country:

"In Chicago, where the most dramatic revelations were made, United States District Attorney Sims appointed one of his assistants, Harry Parkin, to make a detailed report on conditions in the so-called Levee district of the town. In the worst quarters of the town Mr. Parkin found houses where women were kept veritable prisoners. The windows were stoutly barred in these houses, the doors were padlocked and the miserable inmates of the place were practically without clothing. Parkin found plenty of proof not only of the sale and barter of girls, natives as well as foreign, but he found evidence that the sales were carried on under the protection of the police.[268]

If any further evidence against Chicago is needed, we can supply it in no better fashion than by citing Roe:

"Chicago at last has waked up to a realization of the fact that actual slavery that deals in human flesh and blood as a marketable commodity exists in terrible magnitude in the city to-day. It is slavery, real slavery, that we are fighting. The term 'white slave' isn't a misnomer or a sensational term conjured up by sensational newspapers. The words describe what they stand for. The

---

[267] E. A. Bell, *op. cit.*, p. 58.
[268] T. A. Bingham, *op. cit.*, p. 33.

white slave of Chicago is a slave as much as the Negro was before the Civil War, as the African is in the Belgian districts of the Congo; as much as any people are slaves who are owned, flesh and bone, body and soul, by another person, and who can be sold at any time and place and for any price at that person's will. That is what slavery is, and that is the condition of hundreds, yes, of thousands, of girls in Chicago at present." [269]

To conclude this matter of the literal "slavery" of these exploited girls, allow me once again to quote E. W. Sims at some length, not only for what he can tell us in this connection, but also for some very revealing data he presents on the daily routine of the white slave:

"If there are any who are inclined to feel that the term 'white slave' is a little overdrawn, a little exaggerated, let them decide on that point after considering this statement: 'Among the "white slaves" captured in raids since the appearance of my first article is a girl who is now about eighteen years of age... [She was imported from France at the age of fourteen.] ...

" 'On arriving in Chicago she was taken to the house of ill-fame to which she had been sold by the procurer. There this child of fourteen was quickly and unceremoniously "broken in" to the hideous life of depravity for which she had been entrapped. The white slaver who sold her was able to drive a most profitable bargain, for she was rated as uncommonly attractive. In fact, he made her life of shame a perpetual source of income, and when —not long ago—he was captured and indicted for the

[269] E. N. Law, *op. cit.*, p. 143.

transportation of other girls, this girl was used as the agency of providing him with $2,000 for his defense.

"'But let us look for a moment at the mentionable facts of this child's daily routine of life and see if such an existence justifies the use of the term "slavery." After she had furnished a night of servitude to the brutal passions of vile frequenters of the place, she was then compelled each night to put off her tawdry costume, array herself in the garb of a scrub-woman and, on her hands and knees, scrub the house from top to bottom. No weariness, no exhaustion, ever excused her from this drudgery, which was a full day's work for a strong woman.

"'After her scrubbing was done she was allowed to go to her chamber and sleep—locked in her room to prevent her possible escape—until the orgies of the next day, or rather night, began. She was allowed no liberties, no freedom, and in the two and a half years of her slavery in this house she was not even given one dollar to spend for her own comfort or pleasure. The legal evidence shows that during this period of slavery she earned for those who owned her not less than eight thousand dollars—and probably ten thousand dollars!'

"If this is not slavery, I have no definition for it.

"Let me make it entirely clear that the white slave is an actual prisoner. She is under the most constant surveillance, both by the keeper to whom she is 'let' and by the procurer who owns her. Not until she has lost all possible desire to escape is she given any liberty." [270]

The rigors of the white slave's existence are graphically

[270] *Ibid.,* pp. 155-157.

and tragically demonstrated by the fact that the average life of these women caught in the traffic is but five to seven years.[271] The undesirability of the life is further borne out by the quite general joy of the girls who are freed from the houses by police action, and even when circumstances have entailed their confinement in jail (as being held for witnesses) they have practically without fail given unmistakable evidence that imprisonment was a welcome liberation from white slavery.[272]

What may possibly be accepted as the most authentic data available concerning the mode of life of women under bondage to white slavers, are the confessions or reports of actual white slaves. Of these we have not a few scattered through the literature on the subject, but many of them are worthless for our purpose in that they combine a maximum of hysteria with a minimum of detail. However, permit me to present one which I feel is of especial value in that it originates from a woman who was arrested as a procuress, but who had first been tricked into a house (when still a virtuous woman) by the proprietor and coerced into being his personal "slave" and a sort of superintendent over the girls in the house. She was later induced to do a bit of procuring, which led to her undoing. Consequently her position was such as to allow her to form rather a balanced estimate of all phases of the traffic.

"I am asked to say whether the unfortunate girls in these places are slaves in the sense that they cannot get

[271] C. G. Roe, *The Great War on White Slavery*, p. 171.
[272] E. N. Law, *op. cit.*, pp. 158-159.

away. My answer to that must depend upon your interpretation of 'cannot.'

"In my own case there never was a time when I could not have walked out of the building, had I chosen to do so, but my promised salary was always in arrears and I was penniless, with nowhere to go and no friends.

"To walk out on a winter's day into the streets of Chicago with nothing with which to buy a meal and no shelter and no friends under the wide, pitiless sky, is a heroic course to which some resolute Spartan matron might be driven in protection of her virtue, but it's a course which can hardly be expected from a mistreated, deluded, ignorant, disgraced, modern American girl.

"And it must be understood that my situation was very different from that of the 'girls.' I was in the position of a superintendent. They were under me. What would have been possible for me was practically impossible for them.

"To begin with: No inmate of these vice dens is allowed to have clothing with which she could appear on the street. It is taken away from her by fraud or by force, as soon as she arrives, and is locked up. She never sees it until she is regarded as thoroughly trustworthy and sure to come back if she gets out.

"Then, too, she is in debt. As soon as she arrives at the house, an account is opened with her, although, perhaps, she never sees the books. She is charged with the railroad fare that has been paid to bring her to the city; she is charged with the price that has been paid for her to the thief who betrayed and stole her; she is charged for the alleged garments that are given her in exchange for her clothing—charged four times the price that they cost.

"Of course, the police will tell you nowadays that the old debt system has been abolished, and that girls are not allowed to be in debt to the house where they are kept, and it may be that a sort of fiction is maintained, by which, if an investigation were forced, the dive keeper would pretend to be an agent for the storekeeper that sells the supplies. But the condition of debt is none the less real, although as always it be fraudulent. The dive keeper, the storekeeper, and the police are all in partnership in it.

"Of course, it is not lawful to keep a girl a prisoner because she happens to be in debt, but she is made to believe that it is. She is told strange stories about laws that are enacted for the government of her 'class,' and she recognizes, all too plainly, the power of the arm of the police always outstretched in behalf of the dive keeper.

"Police officers come and go in the dive. They register all 'inmates' upon arrival and give formal, though, of course, unlawful, sanction to the business. If a girl becomes refractory and the dive keeper threatens her with the vengeance of the police, she has every reason to believe that the threat is well founded, whether it is or not.

"If, in spite of all this, a girl should be brave enough or rash enough to try to make her way out of the dive, and escape, almost nude, as she is kept, into the street, perhaps she would be allowed to go. Perhaps, too, the police might not bring her back, but they certainly would not assist her escape; and if they did not force her back into the den from which she has escaped they would certainly send her to prison.

"I have seen dozens of girls who wanted to get out from these dives, wanted to leave the life that they were living, but who, under the conditions that I have enumerated, did not—I think I may fairly say—could not do it."[273]

Though it would be quite possible to offer dozens of other interesting stories told by white slaves of their lot, one more, I believe, will suffice. This one gives information on various aspects of the traffic worth noting, and its conclusion is amusing in that it shows obvious signs of prompting or doctoring so as to make it more adaptable for use as propaganda.

"I want you to know everything I have witnessed in my three years of slavery. I was first sold in Custom House Place, by a young man working for Mr. ——, traveling the city and little towns, or wherever he could find girls.

"Here we are, always from fifteen to eighteen girls, most of us very young. The man who bought me made us work like real slaves and then never gave us our money even if it was shamefully earned. His place was always full of so-called detectives, and if some one came to claim some one of us, quick she was slipped to some other town.

"Pictures of foreign girls would arrive by mail, and if one was pretty enough they would wire to Paris and say, 'Send parcel at once.' They arrive by different ports

[273] C. G. Roe, *Panders and Their White Slaves*, pp. 73-76.

—New York, Boston, Quebec, San Francisco—and those poor unfortunates are all claimed by some one pretending to be an aunt, or father, or husband.

"Letters are received by the resort keepers from all the states, and I believe from all the prisons of the world. If any one could read all of those men's mail, I think one would learn horrible things.

"Also we never can receive our mail direct, for the keeper opens the letters, and if they are indifferent they are closed and given to us, but if they are any way wrong in his eyes we never see them.

"If we escape and insist on not returning, they will send some one after us to propose that we leave for Denver, San Francisco, China or Panama. Most of those men who make their living off those girls are old thieves and gamblers, and most of them have served terms in prison. There are very few girls who would tell, for those bad men surely would kill them if they found out who gave them away.

"If one girl is a good money-maker, they make her take one of those men to support. They say if she does not do this, she is not respected by her class of people. They take all those poor girls' money every night, and they send them back to work the next day penniless. If they should not make enough for them they are beaten, and sometimes killed.

"When those runners bring us to those houses, they keep us sometimes weeks to teach us what to say in case the police or some one would try to rescue us, and with the threat to kill us if ever we would tell.

"Some one ought to do his duty and make war on those horrid men. They simply take girls for their slaves in all the country. For even if we are weak, some one with courage ought to help us not to be persuaded by those men.

"I am certainly glad that not all the men are bad, that some one takes our part. You can be sure that most of the girls are happy that some one came to make us strong.

"Have courage! God is with you, and many of the slaves." [274]

Since white slavery, though largely practised in houses of prostitution, is not entirely confined to them but is to some extent in the hands of pimps, it seems fitting to close this section with two accounts of the typical, cruel treatment accorded by the pimp to his woman. The first portrays the immeasurable selfishness and abysmal lack of feeling of the man, as well as the poor return reaped personally by these women who are daily, hourly, constrained to "sell their souls":

"On June 26, 1912, five pimps were playing cards in a restaurant on Seventh Avenue [New York]. The day was very hot. During the afternoon the girl who was 'hustling' for one of them came into the restaurant wearing a heavy velvet suit. The wife of the proprietor asked: 'What are you doing, wearing a suit like that in this kind of weather?' She replied that though she was bringing home eight, ten, and twelve dollars every night, she could not afford a new dress. 'He needs it for gambling,' she said, pointing to her pimp. Leaving the table in anger he de-

[274] E. A. Bell, op. cit., pp. 77-78.

liberately slapped her in the face: 'Didn't you pay $32 for that suit?' he said. 'What more do you want?' " [275]

But the ultimate in callous brutality is probably depicted in the following instance of a man's exploitation of his wife:

"One man who married a woman and forced her into prostitution, used to take her about the Mexican labor camps. He would strip her and put her into a box car to which he charged admission for Mexican and Negro laborers. In one case, the girl several times broke away from her exploiter, but was each time brought back. On each occasion she received a severe beating and finally when the pimp threatened to kill her she again ran away and escaped, but was caught and severely slashed about the arms and face with a razor. This necessitated her transfer to a hospital. One hundred and eight stitches were required to close her wounds. Upon recovering, she again came under the man's influence and resumed soliciting on the street." [276]

Naturally, the control of individual women by pimps was subject to such a variety of factors, its being scarcely possible for any two of them to operate under identical circumstances, that it is difficult to draw any generalizations about their treatment or mode of life, changing so as it did from case to case.[277] In the houses the treatment of the women was fairly uniform in all instances, as we

[275] G. J. Kneeland, *op. cit.*, p. 90.
[276] H. B. Woolston, *op. cit.*, p. 167.
[277] For further stories of girls held by a man to "hustling" and having to turn over all their earnings to him, see *The Market*

have seen, because there the girls became part of a machine and were handled in the mass. However, whether in a house or under a pimp, the existence of the white slave was so uniformly drab, bestial, monotonous, arduous, and above all so little remunerative, that it in itself proves conclusively that her condition must have been that of a slave, for under no other circumstances would a human being endure such a life.

6. *The Fight Against White Slavery*

Anti-white slavery agitation, apparently, had its first serious beginnings in England, chiefly in London, around the middle of last century. Conditions in London at that time were simply terrible: rape, seduction, procurement, and the like, daily went on unhampered under the thinnest of covers. Things eventually became so bad, the abuses so flagrant, the evils so crying, that the better class of people began to protest and take action instead of merely retiring within their own circle and ignoring what was alarming about them, as is the common practise of "good" people the world over. One of the early organized vice investigations, which became so profuse in the twentieth century, was that carried on around 1885 by the "Secret Commission" of the *Pall Mall Gazette.*[278]

for Souls, by Elizabeth Goodnow, N. Y., 1910, which is entirely made up of such accounts. See also Clifford G. Roe, *The Girl Who Disappeared,* Chicago, 1914, for more or less fictionalized stories—but built on facts withal—of the methods of white slavers and the struggles and existence of white slaves.

[278] The report of this Commission may be found, among other

The report of this Commission described, and lamented, a fairly well established traffic in girls and women. But there had been some movement to suppress the international traffic in women earlier than this, dating back in certain of its aspects almost to the middle of the century, and in 1875 the Englishwoman Josephine Butler called a meeting in Geneva, to which the various nations were invited, to consider the international traffic in women and to plan action. Our concern here being white slavery in America, the different steps and moves against international white slavery is beyond our present field and hence will not be gone into.[279]

In the early years of this century, before 1907, the laws in the various states, as Illinois, were inadequate to cope with white slavery. Though procurers, pimps, and brothel keepers were taken with plenty of evidence against them, still none of the then existing laws had teeth enough to harm them. About the only way in which they could be touched with any degree of success was to prosecute them for corrupting the public morals under the Disorderly Conduct Act, and the highest penalty possible there was a fine of not more than two hundred dollars.[280] Thus, white slavery was safe because of the ab-

places, in Charlton Edholm, *Traffic in Girls*, Chicago, 1893, pp. 10-65.

[279] For a concise, adequate summary of the moves and progress in the investigation of and legislation against international white slavery, see *Encyclopædia Britannica*, art. "White Slave Traffic." See also *Encyclopædia of Sexual Knowledge*, Norman Haire, ed., N. Y., 1934, chap. XL.

[280] C. G. Roe, *Panders and Their White Slaves*, p. 144.

sence of proper laws under which to prosecute it; the first necessity in the fight against it was new laws.

But the country was slowly rousing and girding itself to fight this long tolerated evil; though laggardly in starting, America in a very few short years went from complete indifference toward, even total ignorance of, the evil to a concerted, nationwide, organized drive to put it down. In September, 1906, representatives of several associations interested in the problem met in New York at the home of Miss Grace H. Dodge and organized the National Vigilance Committee for the United States, thus counterparting organizations already existing in every nation of Europe. This was a start. The Committee took as its field work:

1. Efforts to secure legislation and law enforcement to suppress the white slave traffic.

2. Study of the causes and of methods of dealing with the traffic in this and other countries.

3. Endeavors to bring the force of an enlightened public opinion to bear upon the problems of prevention and suppression of the traffic in women.[281]

The start of the anti-white slavery crusade in America is sometimes given rather a romantic setting; I offer it as it was given recently by a popular writer, without being able either to vouch for or deny its authenticity:

"About the beginning of this century, in Chicago, a policeman was walking his beat and picked up a note that had been flung to the sidewalk from an upper window. It said: 'Help me—I am held captive as a white slave.' A

[281] O. E. Janney, *op. cit.*, pp. 122-126.

raid revealed the case of a girl who was being held in a locked room, where men visited her, against her will. It came to the attention of Clifford G. Roe, the energetic young assistant prosecutor in charge of vice cases.

"That note became celebrated, and so did Roe. This was the first time the term 'white slavery' had been used,[282] and it flashed all over the country, greatly inflaming people's imaginations. Out of it came the Illinois and other State laws against pandering,[283] and also the Federal act introduced by the Illinois congressman, Mann, prohibiting the transportation of women for immoral purposes in interstate commerce.[284] Roe became the best known crusader against 'white slavery,' starting with that note."[285]

America became white slavery-conscious almost overnight, so to speak. The years 1909, 1910, and 1911 mark the high spots of the great awakening, with interest continuing to run high for several years following. Naturally, this sudden arousal from lethargy in many cases overshot its mark and ran into hysteria. It is interesting to look over the great number of rabid, verbosely hysterical anti-white slavery, and anti-vice in general, books that have appeared in this country during this century (and, indeed, there are not a few of them) and to note that the

---

[282] See section 1 of this chapter for the probable real origin of the term *white slavery*.

[283] See Appendix D for the Illinois Pandering Act.

[284] See Appendix E for the Mann Act.

[285] E. J. Hopkins, *"White Slaves" Under the New Morals*, in *Sunday Mirror*, Sept. 23, 1934, magazine section, p. 15.

great majority of them bear the publication date of 1910. And of all years, it is probably this one that may be chosen as the highest spot in American anti-white slavery agitation, fittingly climaxed by the passage of the well-intentioned but badly bungled Mann Act.[286]

The Federal Government, as is its wont, was somewhat slow in taking cognizance of the problem. True, around the beginning of this century the trade in foreign girls had assumed such proportions that on July 25, 1902, the French Government issued invitations to sixteen different nations to assemble in Paris to draft an international treaty to protect women and girls from the white slave traffic. On May 18, 1904, ten of the nations ratified this treaty, later followed by five others. This country became an adherent to the agreement by resolution of the United States Senate on March 1, 1905, but for various reasons the provisions of the treaty were not put into effect in this country for some time. But slowly the government was becoming aware of the reality of the evil. Congress, by special act of February 20, 1907, created a Commission to conduct an investigation into the subject of immigration, with special reference to the matter of the importation of women for immoral purposes, and the very thoroughgoing report they presented some two years later did much to enlighten both the American people and government on the true circumstances of white slavery in our country. At length, the international treaty, having lain dormant since 1905, was adhered to

[286] H. B. Woolston, *op. cit.*, p. 159; Leo Markun, *Mrs. Grundy*, pp. 604-605; T. A. Bingham, *op. cit.*, pp. 14, 19-20.

by the President of the United States, Theodore Roosevelt, on June 6, 1908, and was officially proclaimed by him on June 15 of the same year.[287]

Possibly the foremost figure in the fight against white slavery in America was Clifford Griffith Roe, who was assistant State's Attorney in Illinois from 1906 to 1909. He started his campaign against the traffic in women in Chicago, but it soon became nation-wide in scope. Though, as has been previously pointed out, he did not invent the term "white slavery," he undoubtedly played a leading part in its popularization in this country. He wrote a number of books on the subject, toured the country lecturing on, and against, vice conditions, was instrumental in having laws passed to suppress pandering and white slavery, served as special prosecutor against panders in Illinois from 1909 to 1911, and was brought to New York by Rockefeller, Jr., from 1911 to 1912 to head the vice investigation committee there. He was connected with and active in various anti-vice organizations and leagues, several of which he himself had instigated, chief among them being the Illinois Vigilance Association, formed on February 10, 1908. His was indeed a busy life; he was but 58 years old when he died recently on June 28, 1934.[288]

The first law proposed in an attempt to get at white slavery was a bill presented to the Illinois legislature in 1908 known as the Juul Bill, designed to punish persons

[287] H. B. Woolston, *op. cit.*, p. 171; C. G. Roe, *Panders and Their White Slaves*, p. 207; *The Great War on White Slavery*, p. 14.
[288] *New York Times*, June 28, 1934.

placing girls or women in disorderly resorts or using their influence to keep them there. Before this bill was ever passed its inadequacies were recognized, even by the people who had been instrumental in its drafting. However, as the bill seemed to have the good will of the legislature and the Speaker of the House, it was decided, after some debate on the part of persons and organizations interested, to let it go through, eliminating certain objectionable amendments that had been appended and introducing some slight changes. With all its defects, it was felt, this legislation would be better than none at all and could constitute an entering wedge and foundation for a substitute bill that would be presented to the legislature the following year. The bill passed the House unanimously on May 5 and became effective on July 1, thus making Illinois the pioneer state in passing a pandering law directed at the traffic in women. The following year, the various organizations and agencies, led chiefly by Roe, succeeded in having the legislature pass the Illinois Pandering Act,[289] which went into effect July 1, 1909. A supplementary act, drawn up by H. A. Parkin, designed to prevent the keeping of girls in immoral houses under the "debt system," was also successfully put through.[290]

In New York, meanwhile, white slave agitation had bit by bit been stirring. The traffic had long been sheltered and fostered by Tammany, but gradually repeated charges against and exposures of this party had so aroused

[289] See Appendix D for this Act.
[290] C. G. Roe, *Panders and Their White Slaves*, pp. 150-155.

feeling against it that it suffered heavily in the 1909 elections. Obviously, Tammany had to clear its name, or at least make a successful pretense at so doing. Of course, the white-slavery charges against Tammany were of small moment (so it was implied); it was the smirching of the fair name of the city of New York that mattered. The only thing left to be done was to have made a special investigation of conditions, an investigation that would disprove all the charges and cleanse the city's reputation, and incidentally restore some of Tammany's lost dignity and standing. A special Grand Jury would be empaneled charged with making a thorough inquiry into the white slave traffic in New York City.

On January 3, 1910, the Hon. Thomas C. O'Sullivan, Judge of the Court of General Sessions, in and for the City and County of New York, charged a special Grand Jury with inquiring into the existence of an *organized* traffic in women in that city. The foreman of this Grand Jury was John D. Rockefeller, Jr., who, though at first reluctant to assume that position, discharged his duties with admirable sincerity and thoroughness, even offering to advance money for the expenses of investigation.

The path of this Grand Jury was anything but smooth. First of all, Judge O'Sullivan was elected to his position in 1905 on a Tammany ticket, and before that he had at different times been counsel for the contracting company of C. F. Murphy, leader of Tammany Hall, a State Senator, a Tammany Assemblyman, and an active Tammany worker for years. Furthermore, every move or action planned by the Grand Jury was broadcast through the city before ever it could be executed; every edition of the newspapers shouted threats and warnings of the Grand Jury's intentions, thus giving the white slavers ample opportunity to cover up and move out of danger's way.

All that winter and the following spring the Grand Jury continued its efforts. Throughout, it was insisted by Judge O'Sullivan that the sole point of issue was the presence or absence of a *formal, organized, corporate body* of men who were associated in the business of trafficking in women. The body could not be an *informal* organization, but had to be a formal one, such as could be got at with indictments; nothing less would interest Judge O'Sullivan.

On June 9, 1910, the Grand Jury attempted to offer a presentment of its findings and be discharged. Judge O'Sullivan refused to receive it, saying to Mr. Rockefeller: "I will receive nothing but indictments." He gave the Grand Jury an additional two weeks in which to reconsider or amend the presentment, and ordered them to continue in session for two more weeks.

On June 23, 1910, the Grand Jury re-assembled and again asked to file its presentment. This time Judge O'Sullivan did receive it,[291] and after addressing the Grand Jury in an elaborately prepared and quite lengthy

[291] For a transcript of the court proceedings during the presenting of the Rockefeller Grand Jury findings, see C. G. Roe, *The Great War on White Slavery*, pp. 220-227. For the presentment of the Grand Jury, see Appendix H.

200 § SEXUAL SLAVERY

speech, thanking the members profusely for their services, he discharged it with the observation:

"Your answer to the main question submitted to you is a merited rebuke to the slanderers of the cleanest great city in the world."

This "main question" was, of course, the existence of a *formally organized body* of white slavers. The Grand Jury, naturally, could discover no such body—the sheer impossibility of such a thing is at once apparent to any intelligent person—and so reported, but immediately amended this statement by describing the operations of a vast chain of panders, in a strict sense working individually, but nevertheless quite efficiently held together in effective coöperation by *informal* agreement and understanding and a community of interests.

Judge O'Sullivan studied the Grand Jury's presentment for six days before filing it, on June 29, 1910. Grand Jury presentments are not given to the press until after they are filed, and this one was filed too late to be available for the evening papers of that day. However, so as not to disappoint the reporters who had been anxiously awaiting copy, Judge O'Sullivan himself told them what the presentment contained, with the result that newspapers all over the country trumpeted forth the information that "Rockefeller Jury Reports No White Slavery!"

What a set-back to the anti-white slavery crusade! The next morning, newspapers throughout the country carried headlines to this same effect, copied from New York sources. One of the largest papers in America carried an article with the blazing heading:

WHITE SLAVERY NOT IN NEW YORK

Rockefeller Grand Jury Reports
Allegations Are Largely Mythical
—No Organized Traffic

Newspapers from New York to San Francisco carried headlines to the general nature as follows:

TRAFFIC IN WHITE SLAVES A MYTH

To be sure, the papers soon discovered their mistake and attempted to rectify it; very shortly editorials were appearing all over the country explaining the true state of affairs. But the damage had been done, at least with the great mass of uncultured, unreasoning people; a dozen editorials cannot undo the effect of one glaring headline. People felt reassured and ceased to worry about an evil that had been pronounced by experts to be non-existent. It has been estimated that this misunderstanding—combined with a certain amount of misrepresentation at its source—retarded the progress of the fight against white slavery by almost a year.[292]

But in the long run this trickery profited the interested parties but little. Once discovered and exposed it resulted eventually only in further discrediting them. An editorial in the Chicago *Tribune* of June 30, 1910, the day following the misrepresentation, demonstrates the general tendency of feeling:

"The findings of the special grand jury which has been investigating the so-called white slave traffic in New York

[292] T. A. Bingham, *op. cit.*, pp. 19-26; O. E. Janney, *op. cit.*, pp. 55-56; C. G. Roe, *The Great War on White Slavery*, pp. 216-220.

will hardly seem to the average man to give grounds for the comment of the judge of General Sessions to which the report was made. He declared:

" 'Your answer to the main question submitted to you is a merited rebuke to the slanderers of the cleanest great city in the world.'

"This main question was as to the existence of an organized traffic in women. And what are the conclusions of the jury?

" 'While we have found no evidence of any organization, incorporated or otherwise, engaged in the traffic in women, nor have we found evidence of organized traffic in women for immoral purposes, it appears, on the other hand, from indictments found by us and from the testimony of witnesses that a trafficking in the bodies of women does exist and is carried on by individuals acting for their own individual benefit, and that these persons are known to each other and are more or less informally associated.

" 'We have also found that associations and clubs composed mainly or wholly of those profiting from vice have existed and that one such organization still exists.

" 'These associations and clubs are analogous to commercial bodies in other fields, which, while not directly engaged in commerce, are composed of individuals all of whom as individuals are so engaged.

" 'The "incorporated syndicates" and "international bands" referred to in published statements we find to be based on such informal relations as have just been spoken of.'

"The Judge is welcome to any moral satisfaction he may get out of the conclusion that, contrary to the picturesque report, there is no 'incorporated syndicate' or 'international band' of panders, but that there are individuals in this traffic 'more or less informally associated' and that there are 'associations and clubs analogous to commercial bodies in other fields.'

"Doubtless the judge's legal mind enables him to wax proud and glad over the fact that incorporation has not yet been resorted to by these backward gentry. But the lay mind stupidly fixes itself on the fact that the traffic goes on." [293]

An important piece of Federal anti-white slavery legislation, which was also a product of the year 1910, was the Mann Act, more properly known as the White Slave Traffic Act, passed June 25, 1910. This Act, the drawing up of which was in large part due to Roe and which was presented by the Illinois congressman, Mann, provides rather a heavy penalty for the transporting or in any way aiding, abetting, or causing the transporting of a woman from one state into another for "immoral purposes." [294] Though this law provides a very effective instrument for the prosecution and suppression of nationwide white slavery operations, it unfortunately has proved to be an even better tool in the hands of unscrupulous women for blackmail and extortion, for it has been officially held [295] that the wording of the Act in-

[293] C. G. Roe, op. cit., pp. 228-229.
[294] See Appendix E for the Mann Act.
[295] In the Diggs-Caminetti case of 1917.

cludes not only transportation of women for exploitation, but also for "any other immoral purpose," even very personal and non-professional, non-commercial purposes. Thus, a man who merely takes a woman across a state line to keep an assignation she has given him, though the woman goes quite freely and by her own desire, is liable under this Act. Consequently, a woman has only to induce a man to cross a state line with her for certain purposes and she, by threatening to notify the authorities, can easily extort money from him, all the more readily as the woman is not liable under this Act since it was really intended to protect white slaves. Roe, though active in the formulation and passage of this law, later denounced it as having miscarried in placing such a weapon for extortion in the hands of women.[296]

Though by means of this Act the inter-state traffic in women was made a Federal offense, the actual prosecution and punishment of the procurer were still largely tasks for the individual states. Few states had any sort of laws to this end, and all of these were hopelessly incompetent. Illinois, as we have seen, was the first to pass a proper pandering law. Consequently, an important endeavor of the crusaders against white slavery was to induce the various state legislatures to enact suitable laws in this connection, and during the spring session of 1909 quite good acts, based on the Illinois law, were passed by the states of Minnesota, North and South Dakota, Iowa, Colorado, and Washington.

But this was only a start. The National Vigilance Com-

[296] New York Times, June 28, 1934.

mittee, with the aid of legal men expert in such matters, next framed a "model law" which dealt briefly but competently with white slavery and pandering. Laws of this nature when drafted by persons not entirely informed on all the ramifications of the subject are likely unwittingly to introduce possibilities for loop-holes and abuses (as occurred with the Mann Act), a thing which a proper Model Law might aid to prevent. This Model Law of the National Vigilance Committee was presented to all the state legislatures that met in the winter of 1909-1910. It was adopted, with slight modifications, by New York, New Jersey, Maryland, Virginia, Ohio, and Louisiana. Also, modifications of the Illinois law were adopted by Massachusetts, Rhode Island, and Oklahoma.[297] Since the passage of the Mann Act, practically all the states have supplemented the Federal legislation by passing laws against compulsory prostitution and pandering.[298] The path of the white slaver has become thorny indeed.

And the fight against white slavery is yet not entirely concluded. In the Assembly of the League of Nations at Geneva, September 26, 1934, there were reports on slavery still existing in different corners of the globe, and among them was one on white slavery under the title, "Traffic in Women and Children," presented by an Eng-

[297] O. E. Janney, op. cit., pp. 138-140. See Appendix G for the Model Law.
[298] H. B. Woolston, op. cit., p. 175. For further, detailed information concerning the legislation for the suppression of the white slave traffic, see Senate Documents, vol. 58, document No. 214, pt. 2, Washington, D. C., 1910.

lishwoman, Miss Horsbrugh, which drew applause after its reading. After outlining what had been done in distant lands in this connection, analyzing the causes, and providing for an international agreement under which the exploiters could be punished, it called for an international convention on the subject at large, to be held under the auspices of the League in the Orient, where the traffic now flourishes chiefly.[299]

7. *White Slavery at the Present Day*

It is to venture upon exceedingly treacherous ground to attempt to declare just what is the magnitude, scope, or character of the traffic in women at the present day. For one thing, data on the matter are almost negligible as compared with those to be found from the heyday of the traffic, as well as of its investigation. Further, blind prejudice always operates to befog unpleasant facts when they are immediate and contemporary, whereas when they are safely in the past they can be boldly and frankly faced and admitted, so long as they *are* definitely of the past. Finally, conditions—social, economic, political, international, etc. —have all undergone such a complete change that the whole aspect of white slavery has of necessity been altered. Increased general education has left much fewer completely naïve and innocent girls to be preyed upon; adequate laws exist under which white slavers can be prosecuted; graft in city government, though doubtless as great as ever, has been forced to change its spots and can no longer very securely mix in large-scale commercialized

[299] *New York Times,* Sept. 27, 1934.

vice, and the protection of participant officials is always necessary when organized vice passes certain proportions. However, two statements may be made in this connection with complete safety: white slavery (in the old sense of the compulsory exploitation of women in prostitution) is of much lesser dimensions than it was twenty-five years ago; and, white slavery is as yet by no means a completely dead, or even trivial, issue.

Further, American white slavery, such as it is today, has had its lineaments drastically altered. It at present seems to have its chief center of activity on the West Coast, while the one-time world headquarters for the traffic, New York, has been left—comparatively—free and clean of it. A recent writer (a New Yorker, of course) asserts: "Just now, New York is cleaner in this respect than Chicago, Detroit, or a host of smaller cities, and cleaner by far than the West Coast, where ugly revelations of old-fashioned 'white slavery' have recently startled the public." [300] An even more sweeping statement is made by Captain John H. Ayres, a retired head of the New York Police Department's Bureau of Missing Persons, who declares that in all his long experience he has never come across a genuine white slave case, one in which the girl's condition had not been to some extent volitional. [301]

This is perhaps a bit extreme; it would scarcely have been possible to find data to compile the present chapter if it dealt with a purely imaginary evil, or even with one

[300] E. J. Hopkins, *"White Slaves" Under the New Morals,* in the *Sunday Mirror,* Sept. 16, 1934.
[301] *Ibid.*

that could die out completely in twenty-five years. Nevertheless, the trade in girls and women is undeniably on the wane. It is affirmed that all observers of commercialized vice have agreed that white slavery in America is a "negligible and fast-disappearing evil." [302] Yet more positive is this averment: " 'White slavery?' In the old sense in which the late Clifford G. Roe, nationally-known crusader of 20 years ago, used the term which he himself had coined [?], the thing doesn't exist." But hard upon the heels of this unequivocal pronouncement, without a word of qualification, comes the contradictory statement, apparently with the intention of supporting the former one: "No doubt many girls are tricked by false promises into leaving homes—the police say many such girls come from the Pennsylvania and southern mine and mill towns, where economic conditions are hard—but if they are imprisoned at all it is by debt, drink and general weakness of will rather than by iron bars." [303] All of which is decidedly repetitious of certain phases of the traffic discussed previously in this chapter, recalling that part of Roe's efforts were directed toward securing legislation against the holding of girls in houses through debt, and demonstrating admirably the futility of any attempt to argue the existence of white slavery entirely out of the contemporary American scene.

The increased difficulties of transportation due to the war, the stimulated vigilance of the immigration authorities, and the like, have of recent years undeniably lessened

[302] B. L. Reitman, *The Second Oldest Profession*, p. 189.

[303] E. J. Hopkins, *loc. cit.*, Sept. 16, 1934.

the volume of traffic from abroad.[304] But, however, the report given in March, 1927, by the committee of expert investigation financed by the American Bureau of Social Hygiene, showed that beyond a doubt a traffic in women still existed at that date.[305]

Ever and anon there is a recrudescence of white slavery that meets the public eye, but on the whole these are sporadic, more or less isolated cases, and nothing to compare with the nation-wide character of the traffic of the first decade of this century. Not long ago, Clinton Beasley, using the old bait of fine clothes and good times, enticed from a North Carolina farm a sheriff's daughter, fifteen-year-old Ogalia Barbour, and contrived to have her and two of her friends, Carmelia Price and Josephine Smith, go to New York to his sister, Mrs. Sarah Crane. It was the old story all over again: Mrs. Crane took the girls to her establishment on West 96th Street, near Ninth Avenue, where they were deprived of their clothes, kept locked up, and forced to entertain men,—as many as forty in one night, they said. A letter smuggled out by Ogalia brought her father and the police, and the subsequent indictment of the white slavers.[306] Old crusaders like Roe and Sims would have felt at home in this case.

Then there was the recently broken up San Francisco-Honolulu white slavery ring. Girls were being procured in San Francisco, as well as in San Jose and other Cali-

[304] H. B. Woolston, *op. cit.,* pp. 162-163.
[305] *Encyclopædia Britannica,* XXIII, 581, art. "White Slave Traffic."
[306] E. J. Hopkins, *loc. cit.,* Sept. 16, 1934.

fornia cities, shipped to Honolulu, and there prostituted. Once discovered, this ring was most expeditiously dealt with by Federal agents under the Mann Act.[307] And about the biggest white slavery flare-up of late months took place in Los Angeles, one of the first American cities to clean up its vice districts around the turn of the century. A young married woman, Mrs. Dorothy Oliver, reported to the police that she had been lured to Bakersfield by a white slave ring, held in a hotel, and forcibly prostituted to Filipinos. A seventeen-year-old Los Angeles girl, Violet Merna Harris, who had disappeared from the city, was found and related the same tale. Other similar revelations led to the breaking up of the ring.[308] And all these instances occurred in 1934, in a year and in a country in which it is sometimes declared that white slavery has become non-existent!

And, if it would lend any additional color to the picture, we can bring our account up almost to the very day of the present writing. A news item[309] of March 1, 1935, tells of a forthcoming grand jury investigation of a vice ring operating in New York City, which ring, it is said, is taking a "staggering toll" from country girls brought to the city. The investigation, it is promised, will be surprising and will involve doctors and lawyers. In fact, despite the reassurances, quoted above, of New York's present-day comparative "cleanness" as regards organized immorality, it seems that the police department of that

[307] E. J. Hopkins, *loc. cit.*, Sept. 30, 1934.
[308] E. J. Hopkins, *loc. cit.*, Sept. 23, 1934.
[309] *St. Louis Star-Times,* Mar. 1, 1935.

city is even now (March, 1935) once again carrying on a crusade against commercialized vice. One of the principal figures being prosecuted is a Polly Adler.[310]

And so it goes. Other cases there are, both known and unknown. Just last year, a Chinese, Gin Lem, brought the Chinese girl Toy Fon Lew, the "White Lily," to Los Angeles and sold her as a bride to a wealthy Chinese merchant there, Kack Lew Gee, for $1,800. Gin Lem is at present being prosecuted for a number of things, including white slavery.[311] These scattered occurrences, it must be admitted, do not inevitably indicate the presence of a national evil, but they do show that white slavery still has a place in America other than in its history.

White slavery will quite possibly disappear from America some day, but its final passing will not be very soon nor will it occur over-night; and though curtailed by legislation, its extinction will not issue from that source. Changed, enlightened, common-sense, practicable concepts of morality, the continued "emancipation" of woman, and allied developments and advancements in our lives and inter-sexual relations, will (even if they lead us as a nation to perdition, as it is frequently insisted) eventually do away with white slavery pretty thoroughly by obviating the necessity for it. It has already been pointed out that white slavers make up the deficit between the supply of voluntary prostitutes and the demand for venereal artists made by the public. Under the

[310] *St. Louis Post-Dispatch,* Mar. 14, 1935.
[311] *Sunday Mirror,* Jan. 6, 1935; *St. Louis Post-Dispatch,* Jan. 27, 1935.

altered situation, the supply of voluntary women of pleasure would doubtless be more than ample to meet the demand in the face of all the amateur competition they would suffer when "civilization" had progressed to such a point as to render sexual intercourse an admitted, tolerated factor in social intercourse. In Sparta, where the sexes intermingled freely, there were no prostitutes. A Roe alone is not sufficient to eradicate white slavery; he must be supplemented by a Lycurgus. "White slavery can exist only amongst a benighted and unintelligent though highly moral civilization. White slavery has been lessened, not because of the Mann Act, or the International Congress for the Suppression of the White Slave Traffic, or the activities of reformers or preachers or the severe sentences of the judges, but because women have developed in their social, economic and intellectual life. They learned that they had a right to vote, bob their hair, shorten their skirts, to live and love, and whether the moralists like it or not they have learned that they have a right to have 'their experiences,' 'their flings,' and that experience is a great teacher. They have not only learned to protect themselves from the machinations of the White Slaver, but they have learned that a girl is not a 'fallen woman' if she has an extra-marital contact and is not an 'untouchable' if she has had a child without the sanction of the church and the state."[312] It has frequently been proclaimed that "many hands make light work"—an aphorism not necessarily restricted to manual multiplicity,— and where work is light there can be no slavery.

[312] B. L. Reitman, *op. cit.*, p. 190.

APPENDICES

APPENDIX A

THE INTERNATIONAL
WHITE SLAVE TREATY

[35 Stat. (Part 2) 1979]

Signed at Paris, May 18, 1904.

Adherence advised by the Senate of the United States, March 1, 1905.

Adhered to by the President of the United States, June 6, 1908.

Proclaimed by the President of the United States, June 15, 1908.

[After a lengthy preamble detailing the reasons for the agreement and listing the nations engaging in it and their plenipotentiaries, the treaty follows:]

ARTICLE 1.—Each of the Contracting Governments agrees to establish or designate an authority who will be directed to centralize all information concerning the procuration of women or girls with a view to their debauchery in a foreign country; that authority shall have the right to correspond directly with the similar service established in each of the other Contracting States.

ART. 2.—Each of the Governments agrees to exercise a

supervision for the purpose of seeking, particularly in the stations, harbors of embarkation and on the journey, the conductors of women or girls intended for debauchery. Instructions shall be sent for that purpose to the officials or to any other qualified persons, in order to procure, within the limits of the laws, all information of a nature to discover a criminal traffic.

The arrival of persons appearing evidently to be the authors, the accomplices or the victims of such a traffic will be notified, in each case, either to the authorities of the place of destination or to the interested diplomatic or consular agents, or to any other competent authorities.

ART. 3.—The Governments agree to receive, in each case, within the limits of the laws, the declarations of women and girls of foreign nationality who surrender themselves to prostitution, with a view to establish their identity and their civil status and to ascertain who has induced them to leave their country. The information received will be communicated to the authorities of the country of origin of the said women or girls, with a view to their eventual return.

The Governments agree, within the limits of the laws and as far as possible, to confide temporarily and with a view to their eventual return, the victims of criminal traffic, when they are without any resources, to some institutions of public or private charity or to private individuals furnishing the necessary guaranties.

The Governments agree also, within the limits of the laws and as far as possible, to return to their country of origin, such of those women or girls who ask their return or who may be claimed by persons having authority over them. Return will be made only after reaching an understanding as to their identity and nationality, as well to the place and date of their arrival at the frontiers. Each of the Contracting Parties will facilitate the transit on his territory.

The correspondence relative to the return will be made, as far as possible, through the direct channel.

ART. 4.—In case the woman or girl to be sent back can not herself pay the expenses of her transportation and she has neither husband, nor relations, nor guardian to pay for her the expenses occasioned by her return, they shall be borne by the country on the territory of which she resides as far as the nearest frontier or port of embarkation in the direction of the country of origin, and by the country of origin for the remainder.

ART. 5.—The provisions of the above articles 3 and 4 shall not infringe upon the provisions of special conventions which may exist between the contracting Governments.

ART. 6.—The contracting Governments agree, within the limits of the laws, to exercise, as far as possible, a supervision over the bureaux or agencies which occupy themselves with finding places for women or girls in foreign countries.

ART. 7.—The non-signatory States are admitted to adhere to the present Arrangement. For this purpose, they shall notify their intention, through the diplomatic channel, to the French Government, which shall inform all contracting States.

ART. 8.—The present arrangement shall take effect six months after the date of the exchange of ratifications. In case one of the Contracting Parties shall denounce it, that denunciation shall take effect only as regards that Party and then twelve months only from the date of the day of the said denunciation.

ART. 9.—The present arrangement shall be ratified and the ratifications shall be exchanged at Paris, as soon as possible.

In faith whereof the respective Plenipotentiaries have signed the present Agreement, and thereunto affixed their seals.

Done at Paris, May 18, 1904, in single copy, which shall be deposited in the archives of the Ministry of Foreign Affairs of the French Republic, and of which one copy, certified correct, shall be sent to each Contracting Party.

[L.S.] (Signed) DELCASSÉ.
[L.S.] " RADOLIN.
[L.S.] " A. LEGHAIT.
[L.S.] " F. REVENTLOW.
[L.S.] " F. DE LEON Y CASTILLO.
[L.S.] " EDMUND MONSON.
[L.S.] " G. TORNIELLI.
[L.S.] " A. DE STUERS.
[L.S.] " T. DE SOUZA-ROZA.
[L.S.] " NELIDOW.

For Sweden and Norway:
[L.S.] (Signed) AKERMAN.
[L.S.] " LARDY.

APPENDIX B

THE HOWELL-BENNET ACT

SEC. 2. That section 3 of an Act entitled "An Act to regulate the immigration of aliens into the United States," approved February twentieth, nineteen hundred and seven, is hereby amended so as to read as follows:

SEC. 3. That the importation into the United States of any alien for the purpose of prostitution or for any immoral purpose is hereby forbidden; and whoever shall, directly or indirectly, import, or attempt to import, into the United States, any alien for the purpose of prostitution or for any immoral purpose, or whoever shall hold or attempt to hold any alien for such purpose in pursuance of such illegal importation, or whoever shall keep, maintain, control, support, employ or harbor in any house or other place, for the purpose of prostitution or for any other immoral purpose, in pursuance of such illegal importation, any alien, shall, in every such case be deemed guilty of a felony, and on conviction thereof be imprisoned not more than ten years and pay a fine of not more than five thousand dollars. Jurisdiction for the trial and punishment of the felonies hereinbefore set forth shall be in any district to or into which said alien is brought in pursuance of said importation by the person or persons accused, or in any district in which a violation of any of the foregoing provisions of this section occur. Any alien who shall be found an inmate of or connected with the management of a house of prostitution or practising prostitution after such alien shall have entered the United States, or who shall receive, share in, or derive benefit from any part of the earnings of any prostitute, or who is employed by, in, or in connection with any house of prostitution or music or dance hall or other place of amusement or resort habitually frequented by prostitutes, or where prostitutes gather, or who in any way assists, protects, or promises to protect from arrest any prostitute, shall be deemed to be unlawfully within the United States and shall be deported in the manner provided by sections twenty and twenty-one of this Act. That any alien who shall, after he has been debarred or deported in pursuance of the provisions of this section, attempt thereafter to return to or to enter the United States shall be deemed guilty of a misdemeanor, and shall be imprisoned for not more than two years. Any alien who shall be convicted under any of the provisions of this section shall, at the expiration of his sentence, be taken into custody and returned to the country whence he came, or of which he is a subject or a citizen in the manner provided in sections twenty and twenty-one of this Act. In all prosecutions under this section the testimony of a husband or wife shall be admissible and competent evidence against a wife or husband.

APPENDIX C

NEW YORK EMPLOYMENT AGENCIES ACT

Chapter 327. Section 7 [Passed in 1906]

An Act to amend chapter four hundred and thirty-two of
the laws of nineteen hundred and four, entitled "An
Act to regulate the keeping of employment agencies in
cities of the first and second class, where fees are
charged for procuring employment or situations," generally, and to limit its application to cities of the first
class.

7. Character of employer; fraud. No such licensed person shall send or cause to be sent any female as a servant
or inmate or performer to enter any place of bad repute,
house of ill-fame, or assignation house, or to any house or
place of amusement kept for immoral purposes, or place
resorted to for the purposes of prostitution, or gambling
house, the character of which such licensed person could
have ascertained upon reasonable inquiry. No such licensed person shall knowingly permit any person of bad
character, prostitutes, gamblers, intoxicated persons or
procurers to frequent such agency. No such licensed per-

son shall accept any application for employment made by or on behalf of any child or shall place or assist in placing any such child in any employment whatever in violation of the compulsory education law, known as title sixteen, of the consolidated school law of eighteen hundred and ninety-four, as amended; and in violation of chapter four hundred and fifteen of the laws of eighteen hundred and ninety-seven, known as the labor law. No licensed person, his agents, servants or employees, shall induce or compel any person to enter such agency for any purpose, by the use of force or by taking forcible possession of said person's property. No such licensed person, his agents or employees, shall have sexual intercourse with any female applicant for employment. No such person shall procure or offer to procure help or employment in rooms or on premises where intoxicating liquors are sold to be consumed on the premises whether or not dues or a fee or privilege is exacted, charged, or received directly or indirectly. For the violation of any of the foregoing provisions of this section the penalty shall be a fine of not less than fifty dollars, and not more than two hundred and fifty dollars, or imprisonment for a period of not more than one year or both, at the discretion of the court...

APPENDIX D

THE ILLINOIS PANDERING ACT

[Effective July 1, 1909]

1. Any person who shall procure a female inmate for a house of prostitution or who, by promises, threats, violence, or by any device or scheme, shall cause, induce, persuade or encourage a female person to become an inmate of a house of prostitution, or shall procure a place as inmate in a house of prostitution for a female person, or any person who shall, by promises, threats, violence, or by any device or scheme, cause, induce, persuade or encourage an inmate of a house of prostitution to remain therein as such inmate, or any person who shall by fraud or artifice, or by duress of persons or goods, or by abuse of any position of confidence or authority, procure any female person to become an inmate of a house of ill fame, or to enter any place in which prostitution is encouraged or allowed within this state, or to come into this state or to leave this state for the purpose of prostitution, or who shall procure any female person who has not previously practised prostitution to become an inmate of a house of ill fame within this state, or to come into this state or to

leave this state for the purpose of prostitution, or who shall receive or give, or agree to receive or give, any money or thing of value for procuring, or attempting to procure any female person to become an inmate of a house of ill fame within this state, or to come into this state, or to leave this state for the purpose of prostitution, shall be guilty of pandering, and upon a first conviction for an offense under this act shall be punished by imprisonment in the county jail or house of correction for a period of not less than six months nor more than one year and by a fine of not less than three hundred dollars and not to exceed one thousand dollars, and for conviction for any subsequent offense under this act shall be punished by imprisonment in the penitentiary for a period of not less than one year nor more than ten years.

2. It shall not be a defense to a prosecution for any of the acts prohibited in the foregoing section that any part of such act or acts shall have been committed outside this state, and the offense shall in such case be deemed and alleged to have been committed and the offender tried and punished in any county in which the prostitution was intended to be practised or in which the offense was consummated, or any overt act in furtherance of the offense shall have been committed.

3. Any such female person referred to in the foregoing section shall be a competent witness in any prosecution under this act to testify for or against the accused as to any transaction or as to any conversation with the accused or by him with another person or persons in her presence, notwithstanding her having married the accused before

or after the violation of any of the provisions of this act, whether called as a witness during the existence of the marriage or after its dissolution.

4. The act or state of marriage shall not be a defense to any violation of this act.

APPENDIX E

THE MANN ACT
OR THE WHITE-SLAVE
TRAFFIC ACT

(36 Stat. 825)   [Act of June 25, 1910]

SECTION 1. That the term "interstate commerce," as used in this act shall include transportation from any State or Territory or the District of Columbia to any other State or Territory or the District of Columbia, and the term "foreign commerce," as used in this act, shall include transportation from any State or Territory or the District of Columbia to any foreign country and from any foreign country to any State or Territory or the District of Columbia.

SEC. 2. That any person who shall knowingly transport or cause to be transported, or aid or assist in obtaining transportation for, or in transporting, in interstate or foreign commerce, or in any Territory or in the District of Columbia, any woman or girl for the purpose of prostitution or debauchery, or for any other immoral purpose, or with the intent and purpose to induce, entice, or compel such woman or girl to become a prostitute or to give herself up to debauchery, or to engage in any other im-

moral practise; or who shall knowingly procure or obtain, or cause to be procured or obtained, or aid or assist
in procuring or obtaining, any ticket or tickets, or any
form of transportation or evidence of the right thereto, to
be used by any woman or girl in interstate or foreign
commerce, or in any Territory or the District of Columbia, in going to any place for the purpose of prostitution
or debauchery, or for any other immoral purpose, or with
the intent or purpose on the part of such person to induce, entice, or compel her to give herself up to the practise of prostitution, or to give herself up to debauchery,
or any other immoral practise, whereby any such woman
or girl shall be transported in interstate or foreign commerce, or in any Territory or the District of Columbia,
shall be deemed guilty of a felony, and upon conviction
thereof shall be punished by a fine not exceeding five
thousand dollars, or by imprisonment of not more than
five years, or by both such fine and imprisonment, in the
discretion of the court.

SEC. 3. That any person who shall knowingly persuade, induce, entice, or coerce, or cause to be persuaded,
induced, enticed, or coerced, or aid or assist in persuad-
ing, inducing, enticing, or coercing any woman or girl to
go from one place to another in interstate or foreign
commerce, or in any Territory or the District of Columbia, for the purpose of prostitution or debauchery, or for
any other immoral purpose, or with the intent and purpose on the part of such person that such woman or girl
shall engage in the practise of prostitution or debauchery, or any other immoral practise, whether with or with-

out her consent, and who shall thereby knowingly cause or aid or assist in causing such woman or girl to go and to be carried or transported as a passenger upon the line or route of any common carrier or carriers in interstate or foreign commerce, or any Territory or the District of Columbia, shall be deemed guilty of a felony and on conviction thereof shall be punished by a fine of not more than five thousand dollars, or by imprisonment for a term not exceeding five years, or by both such fine and imprisonment, in the discretion of the court.

SEC. 4. That any person who shall knowingly persuade, induce, entice, or coerce any woman or girl under the age of eighteen years from any State or Territory or the District of Columbia to any other State or Territory or the District of Columbia, with the purpose and intent to induce or coerce her, or that she shall be induced or coerced to engage in prostitution or debauchery, or any other immoral practise, and shall in furtherance of such purpose knowingly induce or cause her to go and to be carried or transported as a passenger in interstate commerce upon the line or route of any common carrier or carriers, shall be deemed guilty of a felony, and on conviction thereof shall be punished by a fine of not more than ten thousand dollars, or by imprisonment for a term not exceeding ten years, or by both such fine and imprisonment, in the discretion of the court.

SEC. 5. That any violation of any of the above sections two, three, and four shall be prosecuted in any court having jurisdiction of crimes within the district in which said violation was committed, or from, through, or into which any such woman or girl may have been carried or transported as a passenger in interstate or foreign commerce, or in any Territory or the District of Columbia, contrary to the provisions of any of said sections.

SEC. 6. That for the purpose of regulating and preventing the transportation in foreign commerce of alien women and girls for purposes of prostitution and debauchery, and in pursuance of and for the purpose of carrying out the terms of the agreement or project of arrangement for the suppression of the white-slave traffic, adopted July twenty-fifth, nineteen hundred and two, for submission to their respective governments by the delegates of the various powers represented at the Paris conference and confirmed by a formal agreement signed at Paris on May eighteenth, nineteen hundred and four, and adhered to by the United States on June sixth, nineteen hundred and eight, as shown by the proclamation of the President of the United States, dated June fifteenth, nineteen hundred and eight, the Commissioner General of Immigration is hereby designated as the authority of the United States to receive and centralize information concerning the procuration of alien women and girls with a view to their debauchery, and to exercise supervision over such alien women and girls, receive their declarations, establish their identity, and ascertain from them who induced them to leave their native countries, respectively; and it shall be the duty of said Commissioner General of Immigration to receive and keep on file in his office the statements and declarations which may be made by such alien women and girls, and those which

are hereinafter required pertaining to such alien women
and girls engaged in prostitution or debauchery in this
country, and to furnish receipts for such statements and
declarations provided for in this act to the persons, respectively, making and filing them.

Every person who shall keep, maintain, control, support, or harbor in any house or place for the purpose of
prostitution, or for any other immoral purpose, any alien
woman or girl within three years after she shall have entered the United States from any country, party to the
said arrangement for the suppression of the white-slave
traffic, shall file with the Commissioner General of Immigration a statement in writing setting forth the name of
such alien woman or girl, the place at which she is kept,
and all facts as to the date of her entry into the United
States, the port through which she entered, her age, nationality, and parentage, and concerning her procuration
to come to this country within the knowledge of such person; and any person who shall fail within thirty days
after such person shall commence to keep, maintain, control, support, or harbor in any house or place for the purpose of prostitution, or for any other immoral purpose,
any alien woman or girl within three years after she shall
have entered the United States from any of the countries,
party to the said arrangement for the suppression of the
white-slave traffic to file such statement concerning such
alien woman or girl with the Commissioner General of
Immigration, or who shall knowingly and willfully state
falsely or fail to disclose in such statement any fact
within his knowledge or belief with reference to the age,

nationality, or parentage of such alien woman or girl, or concerning her procuration to come to this country, shall be deemed guilty of a misdemeanor, and on conviction shall be punished by a fine of not more than two thousand dollars, or by imprisonment for a term not exceeding two years, or by both such fine and imprisonment, in the discretion of the court.

In any such prosecution brought under this section, if it appears that any such statement required is not on file in the office of the Commissioner General of Immigration, the person whose duty it shall be to file such statement shall be presumed to have failed to file said statement, as herein required, unless such person or persons shall prove otherwise. No person shall be excused from furnishing the statement, as required by this section, on the ground or for the reason that the statement so required by him or the information therein contained might tend to criminate him or subject him to a penalty or forfeiture; but no person shall be prosecuted or subjected to any penalty or forfeiture under any law of the United States for or on account of any transaction, matter, or thing concerning which he may truthfully report in such statement as required by the provisions of this section.

SEC. 7. That the term "Territory" as used in this act shall include the District of Alaska, the insular possessions of the United States, and the Canal Zone. The word "person" as used in this act shall be construed to import both the plural and the singular, as the case demands, and shall include corporations, companies, societies, and associations. When construing and enforcing the provisions of this act the act, omission or failure of any officer, agent, or other person acting for or employed by any other person or by any corporation, company, society, or association within the scope of his employment or office, shall in every case be also deemed to be the act, omission, or failure of such other person or of such company, corporation, society, or association as well as that of the person himself.

SEC. 8. That this act shall be known and referred to as the "white-slave traffic act."

APPENDIX F

THE LAW AGAINST PIMPS AND PANDERS IN NEW YORK CITY

Every male person who lives wholly or in part on the earnings of prostitution, or who in any public place solicits for immoral purposes, is guilty of a misdemeanor. A male person who lives with or is habitually in the company of a prostitute and has no visible means of support, shall be presumed to be living on the earnings of prostitution.

1. The importation of women and girls into this state or the exportation of women and girls from this state for immoral purposes is hereby prohibited and whoever shall induce, entice or procure, or attempt to induce, entice or procure, to come into this state or to go from the state, any woman or girl for the purpose of prostitution or concubinage, or for any other immoral purpose, or to enter any house of prostitution in this state or anyone who shall aid any such woman or girl in obtaining transportation to or within this state, shall be deemed guilty of a felony and, on conviction thereof, shall be punishable by imprisonment for a period of not less than two years nor more

than twenty years and by a fine not exceeding five thousand dollars.

2. Any person who shall place any female in the charge or custody of any other person for immoral purposes or in a house of prostitution or elsewhere with intent that she shall live a life of prostitution; or any person who shall compel or shall induce, entice, or procure, or attempt to induce, entice, procure or compel any female to reside with him or with any other person for immoral purposes, or for the purposes of prostitution or shall compel or attempt to induce, entice, procure or compel any such female to reside in a house of prostitution or compel or attempt to induce, entice, procure or compel her to live a life of prostitution shall be guilty of a felony and, on conviction thereof, shall be punishable by imprisonment for not less than two years nor more than twenty years and by a fine not exceeding five thousand dollars.

3. Any person who shall induce, entice or procure, or attempt to induce, entice or procure any woman or girl for the purposes of prostitution or concubinage, or for any other immoral purpose, or to enter any house of prostitution in this state shall be deemed guilty of a felony and, on conviction thereof, shall be punishable by imprisonment for a period of not less than two years nor more than twenty years and by a fine not exceeding five thousand dollars.

4. Any person who shall receive any money or other valuable thing for or on account of placing in a house of prostitution or elsewhere any female for the purpose of causing her to cohabit with any male person or persons to

whom she is not married shall be guilty of a felony and, on conviction thereof, shall be punishable for a period of not less than two years nor more than twenty years and by a fine not exceeding one thousand dollars.

5. Any person who shall pay any money or other valuable thing to procure any female for the purpose of placing her for immoral purposes in any house of prostitution or elsewhere, with or without her consent, shall be guilty of a felony and, on conviction thereof, shall be punishable by imprisonment for a period not less than two years nor more than twenty years and by a fine not exceeding five thousand dollars.

6. Any person who shall knowingly receive any money or other valuable thing for or on account of procuring and placing in the custody of another person for immoral purposes any woman, with or without her consent, shall be guilty of a felony and, on conviction thereof, shall be punishable by imprisonment for a period of not less than three years nor more than twenty-five years and by a fine not exceeding five thousand dollars.

7. Any person who shall hold, detain, restrain or attempt to hold, detain or restrain in any house of prostitution or other place, any female for the purpose of compelling such female, directly or indirectly, by her voluntary or involuntary service or labor to pay, liquidate or cancel any debt, dues or obligations incurred or said to have been incurred in such house of prostitution or in any other place shall be deemed guilty of a felony and, on conviction thereof, shall be punishable by imprisonment for a period of not less than two years nor more

than twenty years and by a fine not exceeding five thousand dollars.

8. Any person who shall knowingly accept, receive, levy, or appropriate any money or other valuable thing without consideration, from the proceeds or earnings of any woman engaged in prostitution shall be deemed guilty of a felony and, on conviction thereof, shall be punishable by imprisonment for a period of not less than two years nor more than twenty years and by a fine not exceeding one thousand dollars. Any such acceptance, receipt, levy, or appropriation of such money or valuable thing shall upon any proceeding or trial for violation of this section be presumptive evidence of lack of consideration.

9. No conviction shall be had under this section upon the testimony of the female unless supported by other evidence.

APPENDIX G

THE MODEL LAW

THE LAW PROPOSED FOR THE SUPPRESSION OF THE WHITE SLAVE TRAFFIC

Based on the law of Illinois and other states. The most important provisions have been supported by decisions of the State Supreme Court.

An Act in Relation to Pandering, to Define and Prohibit the Same, to Provide for the Punishment Thereof, and for the Competency of Certain Evidence at the Trial Thereof.

SECTION A. Any person who shall procure a female inmate for a house of prostitution; or who shall induce, persuade, encourage, enveigle or entice a female person to become a prostitute; or who by promises, threats, violence, or by any device or scheme, shall cause, induce, persuade, encourage, take, place, harbor, enveigle or entice a female person to become an inmate of a house of prostitution, or assignation place, or any place where prostitution is practised, encouraged, or allowed; or any person who shall, by promises, threats, violence, or by any device or scheme, cause, induce, persuade, encourage, enveigle or entice an inmate of a house of prostitution or place of assignation to remain therein as such inmate; or any person who by promises, threats, violence, or by any device or scheme, by fraud or artifice, or by duress of person or goods, or by abuse of any position of confidence or authority, or having legal charge, shall take, place, harbor, enveigle, entice, persuade, encourage or procure any female person to enter any place within this State in which prostitution is practised, encouraged or allowed, for the purpose of prostitution or not being her husband for the purpose of sexual intercourse, or to enveigle, entice, persuade, encourage or procure any female person to come into this State or to leave this State for the purpose of prostitution or not being her husband for the purpose of sexual intercourse; or who takes or detains a female with the intent to compel her by force, threats, menace or duress to marry him or to marry any other person or to be defiled; or upon the pretense of marriage takes or detains a female person for the purpose of sexual intercourse; or who shall receive or give or agree to receive or give, any money or thing of value for procuring or attempting to procure any female person to become a prostitute or to come into this State or leave this State for the purpose of prostitution or not being her husband for the purpose of sexual intercourse shall be guilty of pandering, and upon conviction, shall be punished by imprisonment in the Penitentiary for a term of not less than two years to life imprisonment.

Sec. B. Any person who by force, fraud, intimidation

or threats, places or leaves, or procures any other person or persons to place or leave his wife in a house of prostitution or to lead a life of prostitution shall be guilty of a felony and upon conviction thereof shall be sentenced to the Penitentiary for not less than two years nor more than twenty years.

SEC. C. Any person who shall knowingly accept, receive, levy or appropriate any money or other valuable thing, without consideration, from the proceeds of the earnings of any woman engaged in prostitution, shall be deemed guilty of a felony, and on conviction thereof shall be punished by imprisonment for a period not less than two years nor more than twenty years. Any such acceptance, receipt, levy or appropriation of such money or valuable thing, shall, upon any proceeding or trial for violation of this Section, be presumptive evidence of lack of consideration.

SEC. D. Any person or persons who attempts to detain any female person in a disorderly house or house of prostitution because of any debt or debts she has contracted, or is said to have contracted, while living in said house, shall be guilty of felony and upon conviction thereof shall be sentenced to the Penitentiary for not less than two years nor more than twenty years.

SEC. E. Any person who shall knowingly transport or cause to be transported, or aid or assist in obtaining transportation for, by any means of conveyance into, through or across this State, any female person for the purpose of prostitution or with the intent and purpose to induce, entice or compel such female person to become a prostitute, shall be deemed guilty of a felony and upon conviction thereof be sentenced to the Penitentiary for not less than two years nor more than twenty years; any person who may commit the crime in this section mentioned may be prosecuted, indicted, tried and convicted in any county or city in or through which he shall so transport or attempt to transport any female person, as aforesaid.

SEC. F. It shall not be a defense to a prosecution for any of the acts prohibited in the foregoing sections that any part of such act or acts shall have been committed outside this State, and the offense shall in such case be deemed and alleged to have been committed and the offender tried and punished in any county in which the prostitution was intended to be practised or in which the offense was consummated, or any overt act in furtherance of the offense shall have been committed.

SEC. G. Any female person referred to in the foregoing sections shall be a competent witness in any prosecution under this Act to testify for or against the accused as to any transaction or as to any conversation with the accused or by him with another person or persons in her presence, notwithstanding her having married the accused before or after the violation of any of the provisions of this Act, whether called as a witness during the existence of the marriage or after its dissolution.

And be it further enacted that this Act shall take effect from the date of its passage.

APPENDIX H

THE ROCKEFELLER GRAND JURY PRESENTMENT

Presentment of the Additional Grand Jury for the January Term of the Court of General Sessions in the County of New York, in the matter of the investigation as to the alleged existence in the County of New York of an organized traffic in women for immoral purposes. —Filed June 29, 1910.

COURT OF GENERAL SESSIONS IN AND FOR THE CITY AND COUNTY OF NEW YORK

In the matter of the investigation as to the alleged existence in the county of New York of an organized traffic in women for immoral purposes.

To the Hon. Thomas C. O'Sullivan, Judge of the Court of General Sessions.

Sir.—We, the members of the Additional Grand Jury for the January Term, 1910, respectfully present as follows:

In the charge delivered to us by Your Honor on the 3d day of January, 1910, Your Honor said:

"There have been spread broadcast in the public prints statements that the City of New York is a center or clearing house for an organized traffic in women for immoral purposes, or what has come to be known as the white slave traffic. Some of these statements may have been published with ulterior motive and may have been mere sensationalism, but some are said to be based upon official investigation and charges made by persons who profess to have knowledge of the fact...

"This traffic in women, it is charged, follows two main objects: First, the procuring of women of previous chaste character, who through force, duress or deceit are finally made to live lives of prostitution; second, the procuring of women who are already prostitutes and placing them with their consent in houses where they may ply their trade...

"But the main object, gentlemen, which I desire you to keep in mind throughout your investigation is the uncovering not alone of isolated offenses, but of an organization, if any such exists, for a traffic in the bodies of women.

"You should make your investigation sufficiently broad to cover not only present conditions, but also conditions existing in the past within the statute of limitations.

"I charge you that it is your duty to pursue this inquiry into every channel open to you and to present to the court the facts found by you."

Pursuant to Your Honor's instructions, we have made an investigation into the matters referred to in Your Honor's charge. We have called before our body every person whom we could find who we had reason to believe might have information on the subject. Among others were the following: A member of the National Immigration Commission assigned to investigate conditions relating to importing, seducing and dealing in women in the City of New York; the author of an article which appeared in *McClure's Magazine* for November, 1909, entitled "The Daughters of the Poor"; a former under sheriff of the County of Essex, New Jersey; the President of the New York Society for the Prevention of Cruelty to Children; the author of a pamphlet entitled "The White Slave Traffic"; a member of the New York State Immigration Commission appointed by Governor Hughes in 1908; a former Police Commissioner of the City of New York; detectives and other agents especially employed in connection with this investigation; members and ex-members of the New York Independent Benevolent Association; witnesses in the specific cases presented to this grand jury, as well as a number of other citizens. In addition, the foreman, the District Attorney and his Assistants have interviewed representatives of the following organizations:

The Committee of Fourteen; its Research Committee.
The Society for the Prevention of Cruelty to Children.
The New York Society for the Suppression of Vice.
The Charity Organization Society.
The Society for Improving the Condition of the Poor.
The Committee on Amusements and Vacation Resources of Working Girls.

The Society for Social and Moral Prophylaxis.

The Florence Crittenden Mission.

The New York Probation Association.

The Headquarters of various Social Settlements.

The Women's Municipal League.

The Society for the Prevention of Crime.

The Bureau of Municipal Research.

We also published in the daily press of this city on the 6th day of May the following:

"The Additional Grand Jury, sworn in in January by Judge O'Sullivan of the Court of General Sessions, was charged with the investigation of the truth or falsity of certain statements which had been publicly made during the past few months to the effect that the City of New York is a center or clearing house for an organized traffic in women for immoral purposes, or what has come to be known as the white slave traffic.

"Pursuant to this charge the Grand Jury has been seeking legal evidence on this subject from all available sources. The information which many citizens have volunteered to give has proved in most cases to be general rather than specific.

"Before closing its investigation the Grand Jury desires to announce publicly that it will be glad to receive definite, specific information as to the existence in this county of any traffic in women for immoral purposes from any citizen or official or other individual who has such information. Those who are willing to assist the Grand Jury in its investigation are asked to call at the office of

James B. Reynolds, Assistant District Attorney, Criminal Court Building (within the next week). It will save the time of many individuals and of Mr. Reynolds if only those appear who are willing and able to present facts regarding the specific matter above stated.

"On behalf of the Additional Grand Jury.

"JOHN D. ROCKEFELLER, JR.,

"Foreman."

As a part of this investigation evidence has been presented to us and we have found 54 indictments:

22 for rape.

16 for abduction.

10 for maintaining disorderly houses, 7 of which were Raines-Law Hotels.

6 for the violation of Section 2460 of the Penal Law, entitled "Compulsory Prostitution of Women."

We have found no evidence of the existence in the County of New York of any organization or organizations, incorporated or otherwise, engaged as such in the traffic in women for immoral purposes, nor have we found evidence of an organized traffic in women for immoral purposes.

It appears, on the other hand, from indictments found by us and from the testimony of witnesses that a trafficking in the bodies of women does exist and is carried on by individuals acting for their own individual benefit, and that these persons are known to each other, and are more or less informally associated.

We have also found that associations and clubs, composed mainly or wholly of those profiting from vice, have existed, and that one such association still exists. These associations and clubs are analogous to commercial bodies in other fields, which, while not directly engaged in commerce, are composed of individuals all of whom as individuals are so engaged.

The "incorporated syndicates" and "international bands" referred to in published statements, we find to be such informal relations as have just been spoken of, while the "international headquarters," "clearing houses" and "pretentious clubhouses" mentioned are cafés or other so-called "hangouts" where people interested in the various branches of the business resort. These and the houses of prostitution are also referred to as "markets."

The "dealers" and "operators" are the so-called "pimps" and "procurers," the "pimp" being referred to as the "retailer" and the manager of the houses as the "wholesaler."

The only association composed mainly or wholly of those profiting from vice, of the present existence of which we have evidence, is the New York Independent Benevolent Association, organized in this city in 1894 and incorporated in 1896. This association has had an average membership of about 100. Its alleged purpose is to assist its members in case of illness, to give aid in case of death and to assure proper burial rites.

After an exhaustive investigation into the activities of the association and of its members we find no evidence that the association as such does now or has ever trafficked in women, but that such traffic is being or has been carried on by various members as individuals. We find that the members of this association are scattered in many cities throughout the United States. From the testimony adduced it appears probable that the social relations of the members and the opportunity thereby afforded of communicating with one another in various cities have facilitated the conduct of their individual business.

On one occasion where a member was convicted of maintaining a disorderly house and a fine of $1,000 was imposed upon him in the City of Newark, New Jersey, the association voted $500 for his aid. On another occasion in the City of Newark, New Jersey, where several of the members of the association were arrested on the charge of keeping and maintaining disorderly houses, and one member was in prison, the then President went to Newark, declared to the Under Sheriff that he was the President of the New York Independent Benevolent Association, and entered into negotiations with the authorities in Newark on behalf of the members who had been arrested. We have, however, no evidence of any such instance in the County of New York.

It appears from the testimony of various members and ex-members of the said Association that its membership is almost entirely composed of persons who are now or have been engaged in the operation of disorderly houses or who are living or have lived directly or indirectly upon the proceeds of women's shame. None of these witnesses, in answer to specific questions, could name more than one or two present or past members whose record did not show them to have lived at some time upon the proceeds of prostitution in one form or another. They claim, however, that all members who have been convicted of a crime are expelled from the organization when the proof of that fact has been submitted, the offense apparently being not the commission of a crime, but conviction. It would appear that this procedure is for the purpose of protecting the individual, if possible, and, failing in that, of freeing the Association from criticism.

Finding no evidence of an organized traffic in women, but of a traffic carried on by individuals, we have made a special and careful investigation along this line. Owing to the publicity given to the inquiry at its inception, it has been difficult to get legal evidence of the actual purchase and sale of women for immoral purposes, and our investigators have been informed in different quarters that a number of formerly active dealers in women had either temporarily gone out of business or had transferred their activities to other cities. However, five self-declared dealers in women had agreed upon various occasions to supply women to our agents, but because of their extreme caution and the fear aroused by the continued sitting of this grand jury, these promises were fulfilled in only two instances, in each of which two girls were secured for our agents at a price, in the one case of $60 each and in the other of $75 each. Indictments have been found against these two persons; one pleaded guilty and the other was convicted on trial.

All of these parties boasted to our investigators of their extensive local and interstate operations in the recent past. They specifically mentioned cities to which they had forwarded women, and described their operations as having at that time been free from danger of detection.

Our investigators also testified as to the methods and means used by these people in replenishing the supply of women and in entrapping innocent girls.

Quoting again from Your Honor's charge:

"This traffic in women, it is charged, follows two main objects: First, the procuring of women of previous chaste character, who through force, duress or deceit are finally made to live lives of prostitution; second, the procuring of women who are already prostitutes and placing them with their consent in houses where they may ply their trade."

Under the first heading, namely, the procuring of women of previous chaste character, we find the most active force to be the so-called "pimp." There are in the County of New York a considerable and increasing number of these creatures who live wholly or in part upon the earnings of girls or women who practise prostitution. With promises of marriage, of fine clothing, of greater personal independence, these men often induce girls to live with them, and after a brief period, with threats of exposure or of physical violence, force them to go upon the streets as common prostitutes and to turn over the proceeds of their shame to their seducers, who live largely, if not wholly, upon the money thus earned by their victims. This system is illustrated in an indictment and conviction where the defendant by such promises induced a girl of fifteen to leave her home and within two weeks put her on the streets as a common prostitute.

We find also that these persons ill-treat and abuse the women with whom they live and beat them at times in order to force them to greater activity and longer hours of work on the streets. This is illustrated in the case of another defendant who was indicted and convicted for brutally slashing with a knife the face of "his girl" and leaving her disfigured for life, merely because she was no longer willing to prostitute herself for his benefit.

In this connection mention should be made of the moving picture shows as furnishing to this class of persons an opportunity for leading girls into a life of shame. These shows naturally attract large numbers of children, and while the law provides that no child under the age of sixteen shall be allowed to attend them unaccompanied by parent or guardian, it is a fact, as shown by the number of arrests and convictions that the law is frequently violated. Evidence upon which indictments have been found and convictions subsequently secured, has been given which shows that, in spite of the activities of the authorities in watching these places, many girls owe their ruin to frequenting them. An instance of the above is the case of a defendant indicted by this grand jury and convicted before Your Honor, where three girls met as many young men at a Harlem moving picture show. At the end of the performance the young men were taken by an employee of the place through a door in the rear into a connecting building—used as a fire exit for the moving picture show—where they met the girls, and all passed the night together.

The Society for the Prevention of Cruelty to Children has furnished statistics showing that since the 13th day of December, 1906, 33 cases of rape and seduction originated in moving picture shows, in some instances the perpetrators being the employees of the shows.

It is not the purpose of this reference to bring an indictment against the moving picture show, which under proper restrictions may be an important and valuable educational and recreative factor, but rather to point out possible dangers inherent in performances carried on in the darkness, and the importance of the observance of safeguards by parents or guardians, and of the strict enforcement of the law for the protection of children.

Under the second heading in that portion of Your Honor's charge quoted above, which refers to the procuring of women who are already prostitutes and placing them with their consent in houses where they may ply their trade, the grand jury has made a special study of the class of disorderly houses commonly known as "Raines-Law Hotels," the chief business of many of which is to provide a place where women of the streets may take their customers. The testimony given shows that girls who brought their patrons to certain hotels of this class were allowed rebates on the amount charged their patrons for rooms. Upon the evidence brought before us, indictments were found against seven of the most notorious of these hotels.

The abuse which has grown up in the conversion of

the so-called massage and manicure parlor, into a disorderly house, frequently of the most perverted kind, has received our careful study under this same heading. A special investigation has been made of some 125 massage and manicure parlors in this county. Less than half of these establishments were found to be equipped for legitimate purposes, most of them being nothing but disorderly houses. The operators in such places had no knowledge of massage treatment, and in certain cases where certificates of alleged massage institutes were on the walls of the premises they frankly admitted that they had no training in massage, and did not even know the persons whose signatures appeared on the certificates.

In view of the above, it would seem important that these parlors should be licensed by the Health Department of the city, and that all operators in them should also have a license from some approved health or medical authority, and further, that proper supervisions should be exercised to insure their operation for the legitimate purposes for which they are licensed.

The spreading of prostitution in its various forms from the well-known disorderly house into apartment and tenement houses presents a very grave danger to the home. It is inevitable that children who have daily evidence of the apparent comfort, ease, and oftentimes luxury in which women of this class live should not only become hardened to the evil, but be easily drawn into the life. The existing laws for the suppression of this vice in apartment and tenement houses should be most rigorously enforced, and, if necessary, additional legislation enacted.

But of the evils investigated under this head, the most menacing is the so-called "pimp" who, as already stated, while often active in seducing girls, is, to what seems to be an increasing extent, living on the earnings of the professional prostitute, constantly driven by him to greater activity and more degrading practises.

We do not find that these persons are formally organized, but it would appear that the majority of the women of the street, as well as many of those who practise prostitution in houses or flats, are controlled by them and usually pay their entire earnings to them. They prescribe the hours and working places for these women, assist them in getting customers, protect them from interference when possible, and when the women are arrested do what they can to procure their release. While "their women" are at work, they spend much of their time in saloons and other resorts where they gather socially. Although operating individually their common interest leads them to coöperate for mutual protection or for the recovery of women who may desert them, and for the maintenance of their authority over their particular women. It is an unwritten law among these men that the authority of the individual over the woman or women controlled by him is unquestioned by his associates to whatever extreme it may be carried.

To obtain a conviction against one of this class is most difficult, for through fear or personal liking "his woman" is loath to become a witness against him, and without her evidence conviction is almost impossible.

Whatever one may think of the woman who adopts the

profession of a prostitute by choice, all must agree that the man who in cold blood exploits a woman's body for his own support and profit is vile and despicable beyond expression. Only through the arousing of an intelligent and determined public sentiment which will back up the forces of law in their effort to ferret out and bring to justice the members of this debased class, is there hope of stamping out those vilest of human beings found to-day in the leading cities of this and other lands.

In view of the foregoing we recommend:

1. That no effort be spared in bringing to justice the so-called "pimp." When the character and prevalence of these creatures are more fully realized and public sentiment aroused regarding them, the inadequate punishment now imposed should be increased and every legitimate means devised and put into execution to exterminate them.

2. That the existing laws be more rigidly enforced to safeguard the patrons of the moving picture shows, and that parents and guardians exercise more careful supervision over their children in connection with their attendance upon these shows.

3. That vigorous efforts be made to minimize the possibility of the Raines-Law Hotel becoming a disorderly house, and that where necessary proper supervision and inspection looking toward that end be provided.

4. That the so-called massage and manicure parlors be put under the control of the Health Department; that a

license from this department be required for their operation; that certificates be granted to operators only by some approved medical authority, and that proper measures be taken to enforce these laws.

5. That the laws relating to prostitution in apartment and tenement houses be rigidly enforced, and that the present laws be supplemented, if necessary.

6. That a commission be appointed by the Mayor to make a careful study of the laws relating to and the methods of dealing with the social evil in the leading cities of this country and of Europe, with a view of devising the most effective means of minimizing the evil in this city.

JOHN D. ROCKEFELLER, JR.,

Foreman.

GEO. F. CRANE, Secretary.

Dated, June 9, 1910.

www.ingramcontent.com/pod-product-compliance
Lightning Source LLC
Chambersburg PA
CBHW022352280326
41935CB00007B/165